This Is
Your Captain
Speaking

This Is
Your Captain
Speaking

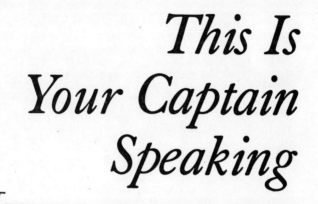

A HANDBOOK
FOR AIR TRAVELERS

Captain Thomas M. Ashwood

STEIN AND DAY/*Publishers*/New York

First published in 1974

Copyright © 1974 by Thomas M. Ashwood

Library of Congress Catalog Card No. 72–81606

All rights reserved

Designed by Michael Feldman

Printed in the United States of America

Stein and Day/*Publishers*/Scarborough House, Briarcliff Manor, N.Y. 10510

ISBN 0–8128–1518–1

*Dedicated to my Indian princess
whose love, devotion, help, and faith
made this book possible.*

Contents

Welcome Aboard

Airline passengers fall into two distinct categories—those who are afraid of flying and those who are not.

Both groups do have one thing in common—an almost total void in their knowledge and understanding as to how and why the airplane they are sitting in can carry them over great distances at speeds approaching that of sound, thousands of feet above their natural environment.

There are few of us in automobiles, ships, or trains, who do not have at least a rudimentary understanding of how our vehicle, vessel, or locomotive works.

The little old lady from Pasadena in her '62 Falcon can tell you that the engine drives the wheels of her car by "turning that gear do-hickey, which in turn causes that transmission thingamibob to make the rear wheels turn." A somewhat vague, but nevertheless accurate, description of the power drive train of her automobile.

Every day, thousands of passengers climb on board airplanes without the slightest idea as to how and why that complex construction of aluminum, steel, and wire is able to transport them to their destinations.

As an airline pilot, I often utilize the free travel opportunities my work allows. Consequently, I spend almost as much time as a passenger as I do "working up front."

In my travels as a passenger, I rarely admit to my true

profession. To do so usually invites a torrent of questions from my seat companion that occupies me from New York to Rome. I don't dislike my work, nor am I ashamed of it. But I, too, like to relax, read, watch the movie and the stewardesses.

On the other hand it is certainly true of flying that knowledge leads to understanding and understanding to enjoyment.

For me, flying has always been a thrill. By reading this I hope you'll discover how to get just as big a kick out of it as I do.

Despite the efforts of structural engineers and interior designers, when you step aboard an airplane you feel you are entering an aluminum tube. Plush carpets, comfortable seats, and the "large" interior windows are decorating tricks designed to create an atmosphere of solid comfort and spaciousness. The actual size of the exterior windows is necessarily quite small. Larger windows would seriously impair the structural integrity of the cabin.

On the jumbo jets, the claustrophobic atmosphere is lessened by the astonishing dimensions of the cabin. Nevertheless, the furnishings attempt to make a quart seem like a gallon. A modern commercial jet is in fact a masterpiece of space utilization. Almost all passenger-related equipment is scaled down in size from the toilets and washbasins to the knives and forks and salt shakers.

Most passengers, having settled down and buckled their seat belts, cannot resist the urge to rummage through the seat pocket in front of them. I know that each time I fly, I harbor the secret hope that I will discover a cache of smuggled diamonds waiting to be picked up by a courier farther along the line.

Alas, as always, I only find the usual collection of materials provided by the airline. Though generally less exciting than diamonds, they do provide something to read, and, in some cases, could save your life.

The airline magazine offers interesting articles and puzzles, and on those airlines that provide in-flight entertainment, a listing of the available music programs. There is also that ominous little waterproof bag with a set of rather unnecessary instructions printed on the side. The next item is a little SEAT OCCUPIED sign, very useful at intermediate stops where you may deplane and stretch your legs but do not wish to lose your well-located seat next to a window, or an attractive man or woman, depending on your gender or personal inclinations.

Last but certainly not least is the emergency instructions card containing safety information for the type of airplane you are on. During the briefing from the stewardess, you will usually be advised to read it at your leisure. A smart traveler will take a few minutes and read it carefully before take-off.

It will show you the location of all the emergency exits so that you can spot the one nearest to your seat. The door by which you entered may be the most distant and least desirable exit should you have to deplane in a hurry.

Most airplane crashes are survivable. However, it is sadly a matter of record that most passenger deaths occur when passengers become trapped in the rear or forward areas of the cabin, trying to exit through their original entry doors, struggling past several clearly marked exits to get there.

Knowing the location of the exit nearest to you can be just as lifesaving an act as buckling your safety belt in a car. Both are common-sense precautions.

During boarding time, the pilots are in the cockpit going through checklists, preparing the aircraft for engine-start. The stewardesses are smiling their way up and down the aisles directing people to their seats, hanging up coats and suit bags, and making their charges comfortable.

If you are seated by a window you can probably see the ground mechanic give the signal for starting the engines. As their whine becomes a roar, a slight tremor makes the airplane seem to shiver with anticipation. Next, the cabin lights flicker. The flight engineer is checking the capacity of each engine's generator to maintain the essential electrical functions on its own if the need arises, by switching the entire system to one engine at a time.

The thump you hear at this point is from the cabin doors being closed. You may also notice a slight discomfort in your ear. The cabin air pressure is being built up in preparation for high altitudes.

The ground mechanic is now waving the airplane toward him as he slowly backs away. There is a slight jerk as the parking brakes are released, the engine noise builds, and the airplane starts to move under its own power. You are on your way.

The public address system clicks on and a disembodied voice directs your attention to the stewardess standing in your section of the cabin. She is demonstrating the function of your overhead service unit, which includes the emergency oxygen system: A nose-and-mouth cup for each passenger will automatically drop if required. On an average flight, I would guess that less than 10 percent of the passengers pay any attention to this demonstration. In the remote possibility that it may be required, the remaining 90 percent would regret their inattention.

If your flight route takes you long distances over water, each seat will be equipped with an inflatable life vest stowed beneath it. Pay attention to the stewardess as she demonstrates the use of the life vest. There have, to date, been four instances of disabled commercial airplanes being brought down on the sea. One had been anticipated and the crew had plenty of time to prepare the passengers. The

13

other three were totally unexpected and some passengers lost their lives because they didn't know where to find their life vests, let alone how to inflate them. On an overland flight, life vests are not usually carried. However, in anticipation of that billion-to-one chance that the airplane may come down in a lake or river, you should know that the seat cushion you are sitting on may be used for flotation. You just have to give it a sharp tug to remove it and slip your arms through the straps underneath it. It is manufactured from materials that will keep you afloat for hours if necessary.

Taxiing out to the runway seems a slow process. Actually, you are probably moving at a speed somewhere between 30 and 40 MPH. The sheer bulk of the plane makes it appear to move at a snail's pace. The larger the airplane, the slower its taxi speed appears. Some pilots have actually been fined by the Federal Aviation Agency for taxiing too fast! Picture a leather-clad, helmeted motorcycle cop leaning on the wing writing a ticket while the captain fumbles in his wallet for his license. During its first week in service a Boeing 747 jumbo jet was taxiing abreast of a comparatively tiny Douglas DC-9. The captain of the DC-9 picked up his microphone and said laconically to his big brother, "Hey, Pan Am, wanna drag?"

Your airplane is now well away from the terminal, and if you are at a major airport, other airplanes seem to be milling around you in apparent disorder. Maneuvering a jumbo jet is like driving a block of apartments from a fourth-story window, and you may wonder how the captain guides his monster amidst all this traffic. The answer is, "Very carefully!"

The wingspan is in excess of 100 feet and the extremities are not easily visible from the cockpit. With the aid of engine thrust, judicious braking, and a small steering wheel connected to the nose wheels, the pilot can make very precise maneuvers. The airplane's excellent brake system can also stop the whole business on the proverbial dime—a very good reason to obey the *FASTEN SEAT BELT* sign. You could make a spectacular unannounced visit to the cockpit if you are unharnessed when the captain finds an urgent reason to stop.

The size of some major airports makes it necessary to taxi several miles before reaching the take-off point. Driving in a strange city during rush hour is child's play compared to finding your way around at Los Angeles, Kennedy, or O'Hare airports. It is not surprising that this phase of a flight is the one where a pilot is most likely to get lost.

Airports have special ground controllers with radio frequencies for taxiing aircraft. I am convinced that this breed of controllers is handpicked for their ability to deliver the Gettysburg Address in under forty-five seconds. A typical taxi clearance would go something like, "Roger TWA 187, you are cleared to Runway 32-left via the inner, take Oscar to the outer, turn left at Zulu via the new scenic route, over the bridge, hold at Runway 09-right, and watch out for a Delta DC-8 entering on your left." Before you even have a chance to say, "Uh . . ." the radio frequency is flooded with noise as the ground controller gives instructions to another flight.

When I first became a captain I often had difficulty finding my way around an airport. One night in Los Angeles, not wanting to show my ignorance, I slipped snugly behind a United Airlines plane and decided to follow him to the take-off runway. You can imagine my embarrassment when I found myself trapped in the United Airlines maintenance area, five miles from the runway. I must say that the ground controller was very decent about it. He didn't pull my leg *too* much as he helped me find my way back.

While getting lost will delay your getting off the ground, the usual reason is simply a traffic jam. All those airplanes you see milling around are scheduled to take off on the same runway. The air traffic controllers known as "tower controllers" must maintain a time lag of three minutes between departing airplanes. If you are number seven in line for take-off you could wait twenty minutes before getting clearance.

There are no priority privileges for take-off: It is a case of first come, first served. A small single-engine light airplane receives the same consideration as a jumbo jet. John Volpe, the U.S. ambassador to Italy and former Secretary of Transportation, tells a story that illustrates the tower controller's impartiality. Ambassador Volpe had been traveling in a small government jet and was waiting in line behind six other planes at Washington National Airport. Being in a hurry, he instructed his pilot to inform the controller that he was on board. The tower controller replied cheerfully, "Our best wishes to Mr. Volpe, we are sure he will be delighted to know that he is number seven for take-off!" (The only airplane that does not have to wait its turn is the President's *Air Force One*.)

While we are waiting to take off, let's take a brief look at how this oversized aluminum tube gets off the ground. Modern jets weigh between 40 and 375 tons. To lift that against the force of gravity and make it fly at speeds nudging the speed of sound is no mean task.

Contrary to popular belief it is the wings and not the engines that are the basic means of transportation. The most important factor in wing construction is its shape. If you cut off several feet, the cross section would look something like a teardrop lying on its side with its lower side flattened. (The boomerang, used by Australian Bushmen, has an identical cross-section.) The front, or "leading edge," of the section would be rounded, and the rear, or "trailing edge," comes to a point.

If this shape is moved through the air with the rounded leading edge cocked up at a slight angle to the horizontal, air will strike the underside of the wing and create an upward pressure. Air passing over the upper curved surface of the wing follows the contour.

Imagine the air which strikes the leading edge of the wing as divisible into two "particles." The particle which passes over the curved top of the wing by following the contour has to travel a greater distance than the other particle before arriving at the trailing edge. To arrive *at the same time* as the other particle, the upper one must *accelerate* as it travels over the wing. This acceleration creates a suction, or negative pressure, pulling the wing up.

Simply stated, the air passing under the wing pushes it up and the air passing over the wing sucks it up. The two forces combined provide what is known as "lift."

Next time you are following a convertible on the highway which has its top up and all its windows closed, notice that the roof top bulges at high speeds. This is caused by the airflow over the curved roof which "sucks up" the material. In the case of either convertible top or airplane, 80 percent of the "lift" is produced by negative pressure.

During take-off and landing the wing's trailing edge is extended (and lift increased) by "flaps": metal panels built inside the wing close to the fuselage. They enable the plane to stay aloft at the lower speeds employed during these maneuvers (approximately 200 MPH versus the usual 550 MPH at cruise). Once the plane is climbing, the flaps retract back into the wing, restoring the streamlined profile suitable for ordinary flight.

An additional source of lift is provided by "vortex generators," inch-high, razor-sharp blades that stick up out of the top of the wing to direct the airflow to those sections of the wing surface producing maximum upward suction.

When turning, or "banking," the airplane, the pilot uses "ailerons," movable hinged sections of the wing close to the tip. Banking means the entire plane tilts in the direction of a turn, much like a bicycle or motorcycle does. The ailerons on the wing inside the turn hinge upward, decreasing that wing's lift. The ailerons on the other wing hinge down, increasing the lift on that side of the plane. As in a boat, a vertical "rudder" in the tail automatically hinges in the direction of the turn to prevent the long rigid fuselage from wagging about.

The other movable component of the tail is the "horizontal stabilizer," or elevator. It forms part of that portion of the tail that is set at right angles to the rudder, and resembles a small set of wings. Like an aileron, the elevator is mounted on a hinge. It angles down when the pilot pushes his control column forward, or up when he pulls back. When the elevator is down, the lift is increased on the tail of the plane, which forces the *nose* down. When the elevator is angled up, the lift on the tail is decreased, which allows the nose to point up.

The engines, on the other hand, simply supply the power to thrust the wings through the air, creating sufficient airflow over and under the wings for "lift." They do not, in themselves, cause the airplane to fly. The only flying machine that achieves flight exclusively from its engines is a rocket. If you put large enough engines on the Empire State Building it would fly like a rocket. Add some wings and it could fly like an airplane.

Chimes alert the cabin crew of our imminent take-off. They take to their seats, strap in, and coolly announce over the public address system that we are all about to launch into the wide blue yonder.

The airplane gives a small lurch: The brakes have been released. The noise of the engine increases from a whine to a roar as the pilot pushes the throttles wide open. Bumping a little on the asphalt, the airplane gains momentum and you are forced back into your seat by the invisible hand of acceleration. On either side the lights at the edge of the runway flash by faster and faster: It is your first sense of rapid motion.

Over the noise of the engines you can hear the airplane rumbling and rattling like a '56 Chevy driving over a plowed field. It sounds like the whole thing is about to fall apart. Well, relax, because it isn't. There are several reasons for all that noise during take-off: (1) airplanes are designed for fast travel through the air, not on the ground; (2) runways are seldom smooth; and (3) the airplane is "flexing" itself into a flying "attitude."

The take-off roll seems to go on forever. Just as you are thinking, "To hell with Science, tonight we aren't going to make it," the nose lifts off the runway. A few seconds later the rumbling and rattling stops: You are airborne.

The long take-off roll is a phenomenon restricted mainly to large jets. Again, there are several factors involved.

At some stage prior to take-off, the pilot makes a calculation involving the total weight of the airplane plus its contents, air temperature, speed and direction of the wind, altitude of the runway above sea level, and the runway's slope, if any. Using all these factors he is able to compute the maximum roll speed at which the take-off may be abandoned and still permit the airplane to stop in the remaining length of runway. He also calculates the speed at which the airplane will be permitted to "unstick" and get up into the air where it belongs.

I use the word "permitted" because long before these speeds are reached the airplane is, in fact, already flying. The pilot deliberately holds it onto the runway to provide a margin of safety to allow for any unexpected condition he may encounter just after lift-off: a sudden wind shift, a loss of engine power, or collision with a flock of birds. This is a "belt-*and*-suspenders" philosophy you will find running through every operational phase of commercial aviation.

A couple of shuddering thumps jerk you from your enjoyment of watching the ground slip away beneath you, but you can relax: They were caused by the landing gear retracting and locking into their compartments. The airplane is now gaining speed and, depending upon its take-off weight, will be climbing at a rate somewhere between 2,000 and 4,000 feet per minute. As the airplane gains altitude familiar objects on the ground grow smaller with each passing second. Above 17,000 feet, most objects are indistinguishable.

Shortly after take-off you will hear an ominous lowering of sound, as if the engines had just died. Within the safety limits of his airplane's performance, the pilot has probably reduced power to prevent the onset of nervous tension, miscarriages, structural damage, and lawsuits among residents in the area immediately beneath the airplane's flight path. Airplane noise is measured and recorded on strategically located decibel meters in these neighborhoods and the pilot is subject to stiff fines for noise-limit violations.

Once the airplane has cleared the noise-sensitive areas, full climb power is applied to the engines. If you are located near the midsection of the airplane, you will be able to see the flaps extending downward from the leading and trailing wing edges. Once they have served their purposes for the take-off portion of the flight, the flaps are removed from the airflow and retracted into the wing.

Almost all airports have prescribed routes that must be followed by all departing flights. They instruct pilots to be at specific altitudes at specific points. The maneuvering necessary to follow these routes out of an airport may take several minutes, but is absolutely necessary in order to avoid other airplanes flying their prescribed arrival routes. To best describe these arrival and departure routes, imagine that the airport is at the center of a number of corridors, some marked ENTRY and some marked EXIT. The exit corridor you are following may not be in the direction of your destination, but it will get you out of the crowded airport area until it is safe and practical for you to turn in the right *direction*.

Los Angeles's notorious "spaghetti junctions" where as many as four freeways cross over one another is no problem compared to major airports' entry and exit combinations. The principal difference is that over an airport you don't have to contend with the unprofessional driver who infests the freeways. Not only does your pilot know what he is doing but he can be absolutely confident that every other pilot also knows exactly what he is doing. All you need to launch yourself onto a freeway is several hours of driver instruction from your Uncle Fred, enough bits and pieces of information to fill a small pamphlet, and a lot of raw courage. On the other hand, to pilot a large passenger airplane, you must endure hundreds of hours of grueling instructions from a hard-nosed professional, accumulate enough knowledge to fill a couple of volumes of the *Encyclopaedia Britannica*, and develop a finely edged set of reflexes and action patterns.

We have cleared the airport area and are now free to head toward our destination. At about this time the NO SMOKING sign goes off (earlier, if the captain is a smoker). Smoking on a take-off and landing is forbidden to reduce the chance of a spark igniting any spilled fuel from an aborted take-off or an other-than-normal landing. This rule is a hangover from the old days when highly volatile gasoline was used. Today's modern jets burn a low-grade kerosene that is considerably less combustible and is carried in craft of much greater reliability than those employed when the regulation was written. I think the most practical reason for not smoking during these phases of flight is the distinct possibility of dropping a lighted cigarette while being subjected to the forces of acceleration and deceleration. It would most certainly roll out of sight under the seats and possibly cause the carpet to smolder or even give a fellow passenger a hot foot as he relaxes in his stockinged feet.

You have just about recovered from the strain of the take-off (with the aid of that first cigarette, or whatever) when the plane shudders and bucks, making the stomach butterflies start up all over again. If you look out the window, all you see is cloud. Again, let me reassure you. The effects of cloud turbulence on an airplane can be dramatic, but are seldom serious.

Clouds are simply bodies of condensed moisture formed by the temperature differentials between heat reflected from the earth's surface and the frontal movement of vast bodies of air. These temperature differentials create swirling winds within the clouds that buffet the airplane as it passes through them.

Approximately 80 percent of the clouds an airplane encounters are between 4,000 and 20,000 feet, that is, during the first fifteen or twenty minutes of the normal jet flight. You may find thunderclouds extending to 40,000 and, occasionally, to a majestic height of 70,000 feet. These are the granddaddies of the atmosphere and are an awesome sight.

But your pilot will do his best to view them from as far away as possible, for the turbulence they produce in the process of their birth and decay can be *very* uncomfortable—for both crew and passengers. To assist him, modern technology has supplied him with an ingenious device, the weather radar.

The portion of the weather radar that the pilot sees in the cockpit resembles a small television screen, on which appears a "picture" of any thunderstorm in the immediate area and its relation to the airplane's position. The pilot, in the dark or when flying through a thick cloud bank, can pick his way around threatening thunderclouds even when he can't see two feet beyond his windshield.

Flying through a thunderstorm area at night can be a wonderfully awesome sight. Great flashes of brilliance illuminate the sky for a hundred miles. Each one of these flashes expends as much electricity as an average town would in a month. Fortunately, most of this interesting activity takes place off to one side of the airplane as your

23

pilot skillfully picks his way through the storm clouds.

Occasionally, airplanes do get hit by lightning. When this occurs, you see a brilliant flash and hear a loud *bang*, which may rattle both the airplane and your nerves, followed by a slightly acrid tang of ozone, accurately described as "scorched air," which hangs in the air for a few seconds before dissipating.

An airplane can even create its own lightning under some conditions. As it passes through unstable, electrically charged clouds at high speeds, it gathers static electricity. This is similar to the way you can build up static electricity in your body on a cold day. When you ground yourself by touching something like a doorknob, you can see and feel the electrical shock leap between your hand and the doorknob.

In the same manner, static electricity accumulated by the airplane will build to a saturation point. Then it discharges itself into the surrounding atmosphere with an impressive bang and a flash. The only effects are that radios may be unusable for a minute or two, a scorch mark and a pinhole may appear on the airplane's outer skin at the point of strike or discharge, and a few more attractive gray hairs may appear at the temples of your captain. Like you, he doesn't like to hear sudden loud *bangs* in his immediate vicinity.

You would imagine that a lightning strike or static discharge would create more damage than it actually does; after all, there are literally hundreds of thousands of volts striking the plane. The reason the effect is so much less dramatic than the cause would seem to warrant is simply that the airplane is not grounded. If one end of a metal cable were attached to the airplane and the other trailed on the ground at the moment of the strike, the results would be somewhat different and would most likely spoil your whole day.

The same principle explains how trolleys work. In my younger days electric trolley cars were abundant. I remember the story of one little old lady who once asked the conductor if she would get a shock if she put her foot on the rail in the road. "Naw, lady," he replied, "but if you put your other foot on the overhead cable, we'd all get one!"

On rare occasions your pilot may find himself completely boxed in by thunderstorms and have no alternative but to plunge through them. These conditions are common in the southern and western states during the summer. At times like this it becomes clear why you are not permitted to stow hard or heavy objects in the overhead racks. In fairly heavy turbulence an attaché case can become a lethal missile.

As the airplane continues its skyward thrust, you may wonder why it takes so much time to reach cruising altitude. Although your airplane is traveling through the air at very high speeds, only a small proportion of total engine thrust is used to make it climb; most of it is utilized for the forward passage. While climbing for altitude, your pilot may also wish to cover as much distance as possible en route to your destination. Depending upon the final cruise altitude and the load of passengers, baggage, fuel, and cargo in the plane, your climb can take anywhere between ten and thirty minutes. The engines operate at high power during climb, consuming about twice as much fuel as they do during cruise. This is, therefore, the most costly phase of a flight.

Brilliant sunlight suddenly floods the cabin as your airplane noses upward out of the clouds. No matter how many times I fly, this sudden transition from the gloom of cloud to a crystal-bright day never fails to thrill me and lift my spirits. And speaking of spirits—this is the time your stewardess appears with the drink cart. As you sip your favorite beverage, the airplane continues its skyward thrust to the cold, thin, upper atmosphere. When the engines' rumble dwindles to a steady hum, you are at cruise level flying to your destination.

4

Getting Comfortable
at 30,000 Feet

We have now reached the social phase of the flight. Your fellow passengers, reassured by the successful take-off and climb, start to move about the cabin chattering with each other. Introductions are made, snapshots of offspring are flashed, and confidences are exchanged between strangers. The fear or apprehension air travelers experience is the great social leveler, and they subconsciously turn to each other for protection in a manifestation of the herd instinct.

But what—if anything—are the captain and his crew up to during this social phase of the flight?

We have already seen that weather radar helps the pilot pick his way through thunderstorms when he has poor or no visibility, but he also has to maintain the right direction, altitude, and "attitude" if he is not to risk a collision.

Attitude for a pilot is the plane's position relative to the horizon. For example, if an airplane were in a climbing left turn, its attitude would be nose-up and its wings would be tilted or banked to the left. When isolated from outside visual reference, all senses are about as unreliable as a two-dollar watch. For this reason, each airplane is equipped with highly sophisticated instruments that show direction and attitude. These are quicker and more accurate than all five senses combined.

One of the first things a pilot has to accomplish when

learning instrument flying is to unlearn reliance on his sense of balance. The primary source of balance is located in the inner ear. When you are walking or driving with visual reference to your environment, the system works beautifully. But when you are flying an airplane through clouds or dark of night, it goes completely haywire.

An airplane in flight "yaws" along a vertical axis, "drifts" along its horizontal, and is subjected to varying gravitational forces, or "g loads." This continual fluctuation in attitude affects the fluids in the pilot's inner ear, causing them to send misinformation to the brain. Because the eyes lack outside visual reference, to correct this misinformation a pilot could be fooled into a highly dangerous situation. For instance, while flying straight and level in a cloud, the pilot's senses could tell him that he was in a climbing turn to the left. If he tried to correct this he would finish up in a steep diving turn to the right. You can experience this for yourself while in flight. Just sit upright, close your eyes, and concentrate on what you think the airplane's attitude is for a few seconds. If you choose a time when the airplane is engaged in a few turning maneuvers, I guarantee that you will be wrong ten times out of ten.

A pilot needs to know several things to perform his flight properly. He must know his height or altitude above the ground, his speed through the air, his direction of flight, whether the airplane is climbing, level, or descending, and if his wings are level or in a turn. He can obtain this information from the array of instruments two feet in front of his nose. His altitude can be read from the altimeter, speed from the airspeed indicator, direction from the compass, climbing level or descending attitude from the vertical-speed indicator, and his wing position from the "artificial-horizon" indicator. This last instrument is a small model airplane within a case that exactly matches the movement of the airplane in relation to the outside horizon.

If the airplane is in a climbing turn to the left, the small model airplane will indicate a nose-up attitude and its wings will be banked to the left.

Once a pilot has learned to scan these instruments several times each minute without any conscious effort and is able to completely ignore his sense of balance, he can function in any flight environment. Reading instruments becomes second nature to a pilot. When driving home after a long flight, I have to make a conscious effort not to stare at the meager instrument panel on my dashboard and get my head up and watch where I am going. During my service in the air force a common army joke circulated: "Take away a pilot's compass and artificial horizon and he couldn't find his way to the men's room."

To the uninitiated, it may seem foolish to allow the safety of an airplane to depend on a set of mechanical instruments. As most of us own at least an electric toaster, we are all aware of the low mechanical efficiency and reliability of manufactured devices. It is a comfort to know, however, that you have more going for you in the cockpit than you do in the kitchen.

Aircraft instruments are manufactured with tremendous precision and care. Most fine Swiss watches would seem crude and clumsy in comparison. Altitude instruments, for example, are examined with minute attention at frequent intervals and each instrument is installed in duplicate, or even triplicate. There are back-up instruments for back-up instruments. Losing all of them simultaneously is about as likely as winning a million dollars in the New York State Lottery, five times in a row. Even with the luck of the Irish, those are pretty long odds.

In the cockpit of an average jet airliner there are more than 120 assorted instruments and gauges, which may be divided into three general categories.

The first group is made up of the altitude instruments I

have just described. Because of their importance, they are situated immediately in front of both the pilot and copilot. Both pilots have a completely separate set that gets its power from a different source.

The next group comprises the engine-condition instruments. A pilot must concern himself at all times with the controlled conflagration within the engines. The main "readouts" are: engine revolution speed (read on the gauge as a percentage of full power); exhaust gas temperature (normally ranging from 350° to 560° Centigrade); fuel consumption (in pounds of fuel consumed per hour); and oil pressures and temperatures. There are even "sensors" that measure the amount of vibration occurring in the engines.

The third group of instruments is a homogeneous array of lights and dials known as "contents and system gauges." These provide readouts on the amounts of fuel engine oil, hydraulic oil, oxygen, etc., remaining at any given time. The "systems" referred to in the third group are the air-conditioning, pressurization, electrical, and hydraulic systems. Most of these are either duplicated or have a provision for alternate readouts.

The pilot performs complete visual checks on his instruments approximately forty times every hour; it is a conditioned reflex that is performed on a subconscious level. An abnormally positioned readout will grab his attention like a warning flag. As an extra precaution, aircraft manufacturers have installed warning lights or bells that are instant attention-getters. Engine firewarnings are indicated by both a warning bell and a red light, for example.

What does a pilot do when an instrument or warning signal indicates that something is amiss? He keeps calm. After all, every conceivable type of failure is a familiar incident to him. During his initial training as an airline pilot and twice each year thereafter, he is exposed to all contingencies in an airplane simulator and practices corrective procedures over and over. In addition to his training, he has at hand an itemized checklist detailing corrective actions to be taken in each type of emergency.

Airplane systems are so carefully designed that there is practically no such thing as a "major failure." Planes can fly and land safely without hydraulic and braking systems. Three- and four-engine airplanes can suffer the loss of two engines and continue safely to a landing. Twin-engine airplanes perform quite satisfactorily with one engine shut down.

Fires in engines and the electrical systems can be extinguished quickly and simply with built-in extinguisher systems. In fact, a fire in a jet engine is no longer the hazard it once was. The "fire" that burns in a jet engine during normal operation is of far greater intensity than one created by a broken fuel line.

Some hazards exist, of course, for which there are no technological remedies. Most pilots would place bad weather at the top of the list. When planning a flight, a pilot carefully studies the weather forecasts along his intended route and destination. If there is the slightest chance that his destination will have less than ideal weather conditions at his estimated arrival time, he will find one, or sometimes two, alternate airports with a clear weather forecast. Enough extra fuel is carried to enable him to reach his destination, miss the approach due to bad weather, fly to the alternate airport, and arrive there with sufficient fuel reserve for a few more flight hours.

There are no filling stations in midair. On flights over large oceans sufficient fuel is carried to either make a safe return or to head off to one of the many emergency airports around the world. For instance, when crossing the Atlantic, if conditions dictate, an airplane can return to the United

States or Canada, divert to airfields in Greenland or Iceland, or head south to two large airfields in the Azores Islands in the South Atlantic. The Pacific Ocean may appear to be a trackless waste on the map, but it is dotted with small islands and atolls that boast adequate emergency airfields. In all my years of commercial flying, I have only encountered one engine failure. It occurred in mid-Atlantic en route from Lisbon to New York. Flying on three engines, we landed in Gander, Newfoundland, where our passengers and baggage were transferred to a waiting airplane, sent there at our request, and arrived in New York only one hour late.

Just so the pilot doesn't become bored, aircraft engineers thoughtfully provide around forty additional miscellaneous gauges and warning lights to take care of radio communication and navigational requirements. Then, for good measure, they throw in approximately 350 assorted switches and circuit breakers. Some of the switches are of such a nature that you rarely, if ever, get to operate them, as they control the emergency systems.

Having already provided us with an impressive collection of instruments, the manufacturers give us one final piece of string to hold our pants up. They install a small battery-powered multiattitude instrument that is sufficiently sophisticated to enable an airplane to use it as the sole reference in making an instrument descent, approach, and landing. I cannot recall an occasion when it has been necessary for a pilot to use this instrument, but it's comforting to know it's there—just in case.

When I was a fledgling I knew an old-time pilot who used to look at me and my instruments with disdain. He would mutter into his grizzled beard and talk about the "old days" when he used the "cat-duck-and-bottle" method of instrument flying. Planting his tongue firmly in cheek, he would tell me how he always carried a bottle of whiskey, a cat, and a duck in the cockpit.

When approaching lowering clouds he would drink half the whiskey to fortify his spirits against what lay ahead. He would then stand the bottle on the dash in front of him. From the whiskey level in the bottle he could tell whether he was climbing, turning, or descending. In the event that conditions got so bad that he consumed the remainder of the whiskey and became so disoriented that he couldn't tell right side up, he would throw the cat into the air. As everyone knows, cats will always land on their feet. By watching where the cat landed he was able to determine his position. When his fuel ran low, he would throw the duck out of the window. Even in the best of weather, ducks hate to fly, so finding itself airborne in such inclement conditions, the duck would promptly dive for the ground and be closely followed by our hero.

Having passed on this wealth of aviation knowledge, he would lean back on his barstool, wink, and permit me to buy him another drink. You will be glad to know that airlines have avoided his methods in favor of more prosaic techniques. It doubtless has something to do with the regulation forbidding pilots to drink while flying.

The regulations regarding drinking and flying vary considerably throughout the world. For instance, when I was flying out of Australia there was a twelve-hour "bottle-to-throttle" rule. One was not supposed to drink for twelve hours prior to a flight. In the United States the regulation states that a pilot must not be under the influence of alcohol while flying and leaves it to the individual airline to fix the "dry" period. In most cases, twenty-four hours prior to take-off is the alcohol cut-off point. I would be less than honest if I told you that this rule is obeyed in every instance. There will always be certain individuals who break rules, but I can say that I know of only a few cases where a pilot mixed drinking with flying. Alcohol has never been found to be a constituent cause of any commercial airline accident; there is a high degree of sobriety among commercial airline pilots as a group. Besides his own sense of responsibility, a pilot is under the scrutiny of his fellow crew members who would be very quick to notice any deviation from the straight-and-narrow. Apart from their professional pride, they have a healthy regard for their own necks!

5

Navigating a Crowded Sky

At any given time, there are more than seven hundred commercial airplanes flying over the continental United States. In addition, hundreds of military and private aircraft are going about their business in the same airspace. It is certainly a crowded sky. An obvious question is: How do they avoid colliding with one another?

Two jetliners approaching head-on have a closing speed of approximately 1,000 MPH. The average pilot is able to see another airplane at a distance of fifteen miles. Only a few brief seconds elapse between sighting and crossing. In recognition of this problem, a rigid system of lateral and vertical separations has been established throughout the world's skies.

The lateral separation is based on standardized navigational procedures and equipment. When flying over land, the pilot must follow prescribed airways that may best be described as "highways in the sky." Like the U.S. interstate highway system, these airways are fixed and are given identifying route numbers. In the United States, airways below an altitude of 18,000 feet are called "low-level airways" and their route numbers are prefixed by the letter "V." Airways above 18,000 feet are, not surprisingly, called "high-level airways" and have a letter-"J" prefix.

Just as an automobile driver follows his ribbon of pavement from road sign to road sign, so a pilot follows a narrow electronic beam from transmitting beacon to transmitting beacon until he reaches his destination. Linked by numbered airways, these transmitting beacons are spread across the world at intervals of about 200 miles. Most of these beacons transmit within a range of radio frequencies known as VHF (Very High Frequency), and have a maximum transmission range of about 150 to 200 miles. Stationing beacons as close as 200 miles to each other permits a good degree of overlap and a more accurate beam to follow.

When flight-planning for a trip, a pilot has to file his proposed route of flight with the authorized air traffic control system through which he intends to fly. To illustrate, let us assume that you are planning to drive from Long Island, New York, to Philadelphia. To simulate flight procedure you would draw up a route plan and submit it to your local highway authority. It would read something like this: "Automobile Pontiac Le Mans, registration number BH 7431, departing Bayport, New York, at 1300 hours [1:00 P.M.]. Standard local to Sunrise Highway, intersect Southern State Parkway to Belt Parkway, Verrazano Narrows Bridge to Staten Island, and Gowanus Bridge to New Jersey Turnpike. Standard local roads arrival to Philadelphia. Time en route, 3 hours 15 minutes. Average speed 50 MPH." You would then wait for the highway authority to call you back and approve your route plan.

In essence, that is what a pilot does prior to boarding his airplane. When he is ready to taxi out to the runway, he calls on an appropriate radio frequency for his air traffic control clearance. His flight plan is either approved or revised by air traffic control, then is read back to him. The pilot again reads it back to the controller, assuring that each has an accurate understanding of the route. The flight route is then transmitted by teletype to all air traffic sectors he will be passing through during his flight.

Once the route has been established, the elaborate system of safety devices comes into play again. Over land the airplane is under constant radar surveillance at all times, from take-off to landing.

Imagine the ground as a patchwork quilt. As you take off from an airport located in a particular "patch," you come under the control and surveillance of a "departure radar controller." When you have passed from his radius (or patch) of control he hands your flight over to an air traffic center controller. This controller is responsible for you while you are flying through his patch, or sector. When you again cross a boundary into a new sector, you are handed over to your next sector controller. As you fly across the country you are passed from hand to hand like the baton in a relay race.

The men and women staffing these control centers are a highly skilled and dedicated group. There is between them and the pilots they watch over a bond of mutual trust and respect. In the United States, controllers are trained and employed by the Federal Aviation Agency, which is also responsible for the installation and maintenance of all navigation and radar facilities.

Being an air traffic controller is no easy task. The initial training is arduous and the visible returns are, in my estimation, small. The salaries of air traffic controllers average only about $15,000 a year. If you find yourself assigned to a busy aviation center such as New York, Chicago, or Los Angeles, you risk your health under the strain of controlling a large number of fast-moving aircraft. The awesome responsibility inherent in the job can and does produce a high

37

incidence of physical and mental fatigue. At Chicago's O'Hare airport, for example, the controllers can only stay at their positions for thirty-minute periods during peak hours. They must then be relieved to rest and relax for a while.

To assist controllers in identifying a particular airplane from the possible hundreds of airplane blips on their radar scopes, each airplane is equipped with a device called a "transponder." This is a small transmitter that can register any four-digit number selected between 0000 and 9999. At the request of the controller, the pilot selects the required code number and presses a button. His airplane's blip on the controller's scope will then show itself as a distinct size and intensity, making the plane easy to identify.

During the early hours of the morning the airways, like highways, are pretty quiet. In the vast empty darkness of the sky the pilot can feel a close rapport with his controller hunched over his bright scope, many miles away and thousands of feet below. That thin thread of rado transmission becomes an umbilical cord of friendship; radio contacts between pilot and controller become more informal. After a period of time controllers come to recognize certain pilots' voices. Because I am one of the few "Limeys" flying for a U.S. airline, it's not too hard to pick my voice out. Sometimes controllers can match a face to the voice because most pilots pay visits to air traffic centers around the country to meet their controllers personally. One veteran TWA captain is known in every sector from coast to coast. As he flies into a new sector and changes radio frequency, his first contact with the controller is a skillful rendition of "Turkey in the Straw" on a jew's-harp. Any controller from New York to California will immediately respond with a cry of "Hi, Herbie, what's your flight number tonight?"—an example of the cool, comfortable professionalism of those engaged in the business of hauling the big jets around the world.

Undoubtedly, you are now feeling more comfortable as you see how difficult it is to get lost flying across the country. "But wait a minute," you may say. "The system of numbered airways and radar surveillance flying may work beautifully when we are over land but what happens when we fly over the sea?" Because of the restricted range of radar and the impossibility of installing navigation beacons in midocean, obviously some other means of navigation must be used for crowded airways over the seas.

Until very recently, finding one's way across trackless wastes was the responsibility of a navigator who knew the ancient art of celestial navigation. He used fixed sun and star positions, drift calculations, and various rules of thumb. It's an old aviation saying that all any navigator can tell you is where you *have* been. A few could even tell you where you should be. But it was a rare one who could tell you exactly where you were at any given time. Celestial navigation was an inexact science at best whose failings were usually the result of primitive work tools and the high speed and instability of the sighting platform.

As with other ancient crafts, "progress" in the form of modern science caught up with celestial navigation. Black boxes replaced human judgment; accuracy replaced instinct. Almost all airlines flying across oceans employ some system of electronic navigation. Probably the most common system in use today is the Doppler system. It is essentially an impulse transmitter and receiver that sends out a fan-shaped signal to the front and sides of the airplane. The signals bounce back from the surface of the sea or land to the receiver, where a computer compares the speed of the returning signal to that of the sending signal. Using this comparison it is able to calculate the airplane's speed. It can also calculate from the reading taken on either side of the airplane if the plane is drifting left or right of a predetermined track. When all calculations are completed, the information is relayed to the airplane's autopilot, which makes any needed correction in direction. A minimum of two Doppler systems are usually installed on transoceanic airplanes, each one checking on the other.

For those of us who still feel uncomfortable with only one back-up system, yet another is available to check the other two. It is called "Loran," a contraction for Long-Range Air Navigation. At various points all over the world large transmitting beacons send out continuous radio signals in the "High-Frequency" range. High-Frequency, or HF, signals can travel great distances, sometimes up to 2,000 miles, by bouncing off the upper layers of the stratosphere known as the ionic layer. By taking readings from several of these beacons on an oscilloscope, a pilot is able to fix his position fairly accurately. Taking this fix and comparing it to Doppler readouts, he is able to check their accuracy. On an average ocean crossing he would make such a check every thirty to forty-five minutes. Very rarely does one have to make a significant correction to the Doppler.

With the advent of space travel a usable system of absolute pinpoint navigation was inevitable: one of the many spin-offs from the space program that has benefited aviation. The navigational system developed is called the Inertial Navigation System, referred to an "INS," which employs a number of very accurate gyroscopes. As the INS-equipped airplane speeds through the air even the smallest drift is picked up by the gyroscopes. They sense the magnitude of the drifting and automatically, through the airplane's automatic pilot, correct the "heading" to maintain a predetermined course.

At least two of these superb devices are fitted to each transoceanic jet of the most recent generation. A nonstop flight from Los Angeles to London covers a distance of approximately 6,000 miles. An error of half a mile "off-track" by the time you reach your destination is not unusual. Don't be alarmed! You would not miss London airport by half a mile! The final portion of your flight is personally entrusted to an air traffic controller and his trusty radarscope.

If all else fails on your plane's flight over the ocean, we have one final ace in the hole to fall back on. Scattered across the world's oceans are small ships from various maritime nations that have a limited area of operation. Although their primary function is weather reporting and rescue they are usually equipped with radar; all have a Low-Frequency (LF) directional beacon that can be received by aircraft. Pilots are able to communicate with them and, if necessary, obtain a radar fix, because they maintain a listening watch on certain VHF radio frequencies. The fix is somewhat inaccurate (maybe within twenty-five miles), but it is a great deal better than being totally lost.

"Ocean Station Vessels" that fly United States flags are operated by the U.S. Coast Guard. I don't envy them their duties. They leave port and steam out to their prescribed position. Once in place, they spend six weeks trying to stay there in the face of wind, storms, and icebergs. I have great admiration for these men and whenever I pass their position within radio range, I give them a call to chat and perhaps break the monotony of their day. Pilots also pass any messages they may have for their parents, wives, or girl friends. A few years ago one of the seamen on board a U.S. Ocean Station Vessel in the North Atlantic was eagerly awaiting the arrival of his firstborn. For three weeks pilots

41

were calling his home in Massachusetts for news of the baby. On the day after his son was born, it was a race among about ten pilots to relay the good news on their way to Europe. I had just gotten into radio range when I heard a Pan American flight ahead of me deliver the birth message. The proud father's elation and excitement was shared by all of us and each was glad that we could perform some small service for a member of that grand crew.

To avoid colliding with another airplane over the water there is a system of "ocean-crossing tracks." Unlike the overland "highways," ocean-crossing tracks are drawn between prescribed points of longitude and latitude, and are changed daily to take advantage of existing winds, and to avoid storm areas.

The daily changes are made by the appropriate controlling authority and tracks are assigned to a flight before it leaves its departure point. For example, the North Atlantic Ocean is controlled from Newfoundland in the west and Shannon, Ireland, in the east. Each locale controls its own half of the ocean. After studying meteorological reports and forecasts the halves cooperatively devise crossing tracks for the following day, and letter them "Track Alfa," "Track Bravo," etc.

Every flight must follow its prescribed road. Because these roads are used in both directions track specifications must include height or vertical separation. This is accomplished by standardizing aircraft flying patterns throughout the world: Easterly bound planes fly at even-numbered altitudes, such as 28,000 or 32,000 feet, etc.; those flying westerly directions fly at odd-numbered altitudes, such as 29,000 or 33,000 feet.

To determine if they are easterly or westerly is easy. Imagine the face of a clock. If you draw a straight line from one o'clock to seven o'clock you divide the face in two. If your direction of flight has a compass heading that falls inside the right half of the clock, you are easterly; the other half is, of course, westerly.

Your true altitude is read off an instrument that operates on the barometric pressure in the airplane's area. On the ground the barometric pressure differs throughout the world. To maintain standardized vertical separation both on airways over land and on ocean-crossing tracks, all pilots during their airplane's climb set their altimeters on a fixed barometric setting (29.92 inches HG). They then fly at what are referred to as "flight levels." This standardized barometric setting ensures that all aircraft are using the same basis to establish their altitude. To convert an altitude reading to a flight level you remove the last two digits from the altitude, measured in feet. For example, if you are flying at 35,000 feet you are flying at flight level 350. This last figure is easier to write and speak if your native tongue is not English. (English is the official airline language and all commercial pilots must be able to speak it with a reasonable degree of proficiency.) Every commercial pilot in the world whether over land or sea flies at these standardized flight levels, making for a safe, simple operation.

You may wonder why it is necessary for jet airplanes to cruise at the high flight levels they do. After all, it does take a long time to get up there and almost as long to get down. But let me assure you there are reasons! Jet engines operate internally at temperatures of about 2,000° Centigrade (about 4,600° Fahrenheit). The air temperature above flight level 310 is usually around −60° C. (−80° F.). Besides cooling the engine components, this very cold air provides a very efficient (and more *economical*) combustible mixture when mixed with fuel.

Then, too, bad weather is seldom found at high altitudes. You are able to fly over storms. Also, above flight level 300 a pilot is likely to encounter a "jet stream." Jet streams are extremely high winds of up to 200 MPH, which are formed by certain climatic and barometric pressure conditions. When plotted on a three-dimensional map they look like a curved cylinder, maybe 60 miles in diameter and 1,000 miles long.

If a pilot can find a jet stream going his way he can take advantage of this tremendous tail wind and have it add to the speed of his airplane. A 200-mile-an-hour tail wind can knock an hour off the flight between New York and London. This brings joy to both the passengers and the airlines' accountants. One hour's flight time thus saved is worth between $1,500 and $4,000. Of course, if the jet stream is blowing in the wrong direction it becomes a head wind and the pilot usually tries to reroute out of it. Subject to the vagaries of the wind, your speed over land can vary between 400 and 700 MPH.

You may notice the ride becoming a little bumpy at times during the flight, though looking out of the window, you see no evidence of clouds. What you are encountering is "clear air turbulence," caused by strong, high-level winds shearing across each other from different directions. Where the edges of these winds coincide, they form an area of rough air much like the rough waters sailors must fight "coming around the Horn," where several strong currents converge.

At this time you will also notice that the wings flex up and down. Let me reassure you: They are supposed to do that. In fact, a wing is capable of flexing through an arc of several feet at the wing tip. Wing flex acts like the elliptical springs on the axle of a car. Without those springs, a car would literally shake itself to pieces within a few miles. This same effect is present in tall skyscraper buildings. They are designed to, and do, sway in high winds. The same is true with wings. If they were absolutely rigid every little shock would be magnified and concentrated on every rivet and bolt holding the wings to the fuselage. A few hours of that and the atoms in the metal would crystallize, making the wing as brittle as glass.

As a further reassurance, let me add that before an airplane is put into general production, prototypes are tested to destruction. To duplicate those tests in the air, you would have to fly non-stop for tens of thousands of hours under continuous heavy shock loads. Although the airplane may appear to be flimsy, it is in fact as strong as a tank.

The temperature a couple of inches on the other side of your window is −60° C. In terms of your thermostat at home that is 110° F. below freezing. To heat the airplane's interior, very hot air is tapped from the jet engines, mixed with cold air, and fed to the cabins. Ideally, the air is maintained at an even 70° F. If you are uncomfortable, you may ask the stewardess to request a change in temperature from the flight engineer.

So much for warmth. What about the oxygen supply system? At high flight levels there is very little oxygen in the air outside the plane. How can you survive without wearing an oxygen mask all the time? The engines are fitted with "compressors." They take air and literally "squeeze" it to a higher density and, consequently, a higher oxygen content. This air is continuously pumped into the airplane. Once it has been used on its passage through the airplane, it is "dumped" overboard through valves. It is as if you were sitting in a rigid balloon that was constantly being inflated to compensate for a metered leak occurring through the outflow valves. The pressure differential between the cabin and the outside is in a ratio of 8 to 1. In the cabin this translates to about the atmosphere you would find on top of a 4,000-foot mountain. Because of the reduced pressure, alcohol enters your bloodstream more rapidly and you could get a little tipsy on just a couple of drinks while in flight. People who move to Denver or Albuquerque (both approximately 5,000 feet above sea level) experience the same effect for several weeks until their bodies acclimatize to the new low-pressure surroundings.

One common concern of passengers is the possibility of being sucked out of the airplane if a hole "should happen to appear" in the fuselage. Well, Hollywood to the contrary, that is highly unlikely. If the hole were large enough you could, I guess, fall through it. The most serious structural failure of this kind that I can imagine would be a window popping out. The chances of such a thing happening are virtually nil, but if it did, you would probably lose only your newspaper, a cigarette, your cool, and any other lightweight object in the vicinity of the window! The pressurization system would have no problem coping with a hole that size and could quite capably maintain adequate pressure. The only unpleasant effect would be a high noise level and varying degrees of hysteria among the more nervous passengers!

If a total loss of pressurization should ever occur at high altitude, the emergency oxygen mask would drop in front of your face. You would only have to give it a tug to start the flow of oxygen, place it over your nose and mouth, and breathe normally. You could sit that way safely for several hours if need be.

Over the years I have received hundreds of requests to "radio ahead" an urgent personal message. Despite a dip-

lomatically worded reply from me relayed by the stewardess, the passengers requesting the transmission inevitably
become very chagrined when I refuse. Personal radio messages are strictly forbidden by international law and although it may seem to be a small and easy thing to violate, I
would prefer not to pay the substantial fine that would be
levied against me!

Airline companies have their own radio frequencies,
and while in range of a receiver the pilot can speak to
almost any point in the world through a series of radio and
telephone "patches." There have been a number of instances when crews with mechanical malfunctions have
circled an airfield while they spoke with the engineers
hundreds of miles away who had designed and manufactured their craft, in an attempt to trace the problem and
find a solution.

As with transmitter beacons, almost all radio communications are conducted in the VHF frequency range because that particular radio band is extremely clear and
static-free. Its main disadvantage is that it has a relatively
short range in terms of distance of transmissions and re-
ception. Two hundred miles is about the maximum range
for clear communication. This short range presents no
problem over populated land masses; you just fly from one
receiver-transmitter range into the next one.

When crossing large unpopulated areas such as deserts
and oceans that extend well beyond the range of VHF, you
must resort to the noisy, crackling band of radio frequencies
known as HF (High Frequency). Although its long range
can cover great distances, it is very susceptible to thunderstorms, sunspots, and a number of other natural oddities.

Recent developments in space technology are ringing
the death knell for HF radio communication. Very soon,

airplanes will be able to transmit and receive clear radio messages over thousands of miles simply by bouncing their signals off orbiting space satellites. This will be a refined version of our present Telstar system, which relays television programs around the world. I envision a time when a flight passenger will be able to place a telephone call to anywhere in the world. In fact, the possibilities for communication seem endless. Anyone who complains about the "lack of communication these days" either lives in the Gobi desert or in a one-telephone home with a teenage daughter!

What about the future of airplanes, and commercial aviation in general? Believe it or not, there are airplanes presently at the design stage that will be capable of carrying up to 1,000 passengers. As a pilot, my mind boggles at the thought of so many people in one airplane. Distributing that amount of weight for take-off alone is going to be a problem. I can hear it now over the public address system: "Will the passengers seated in the first sixty rows kindly run to the rear so we can lift the nose wheel for take-off?"

The motivation behind building a bigger airplane is, of course, economy. The airlines are reluctant to add more airplanes to an already saturated system of airways, and would like to handle the expected increase in air travel not with more flights, but with airplanes of greater capacity. Jumbo or superjumbo jets, filled to capacity with passengers and cargo, would provide the needed additional space. If the traveling public responded to the larger airplanes and filled them to capacity, fares could be lowered and even more customers would be encouraged to fly. When you consider that less than 40 percent of the American public has ever flown, you can see the potential.

We have talked about bigger airplanes, but what about faster ones? Airplanes have been flying faster than the speed of sound for the last twenty years. Military fighters and bombers routinely operate at three times that speed. Why isn't a supersonic commercial airliner already in use?

To clarify the problems involved, maybe I should explain just what the effects of speed of sound are. At sea level, sound travels at approximately 720 MPH. An airplane flying faster than this speed compresses the air ahead of it and creates a shock wave not unlike the bow wave in front of a ship. As the airplane flies even faster the shock wave manifests itself as a sonic boom that will rattle your house like a nearby clap of thunder. Damage to property, people, and animal life becomes a real possibility.

The whole question of the development of an SST (Supersonic Transport) is highly controversial. Not only has it become a hot political football, but the increasingly strong ecology groups have taken an opposing stand. Surprisingly, commercial pilots in the United States also seem divided on this issue.

The advantages are obvious. Because of very high speeds you get from here to there in about half the time. Fly New York to London between breakfast and lunch, London to Sydney, Australia, for breakfast again.

On the other hand, say the detractors, "Who wants to do that?" The costs involved in halving existing flight times are staggering. Many feel that the astronomical development costs for such an airplane would be better spent on improving the quality and quantity of existing surface transportation facilities. Unquestionably, the most frustrating and dangerous journey you can undertake is the one from your home to the airport.

Proponents say, "That's progress. If Orville and Wilbur Wright had succumbed to considerations of cost and noise, we wouldn't have airplanes."

The ecologists respond that the sonic booms produced

49

by such airplanes would cause everything from tension headaches to aborted pregnancies.

My own view is that employing supersonic airplanes in commercial aviation is like using a Maserati for a taxi service. The canceled orders for the Concorde (jointly developed by France and England) suggest most airlines agree with me.

Imagine, if by some fluke, SSTs were used for ordinary flights. The captain would announce as you take off from New York, "Ladies and gentlemen, kindly fasten your seatbelts for take-off. Those of you on the right now have a wonderful view of Lake Michigan. Those on the left can now see Pike's Peak just beneath us. We can now all enjoy a great view of the Golden Gate Bridge on our final approach to San Francisco!"

Sound like fun?

6

Ladies and Gentlemen: The Sunset

Now we know something about airflow, airspeed, communications, cabin pressure, and navigation, among other things. We also know that we have been thrust into this new environment courtesy of the jet engine. Just what is a jet engine and how does it work?

Probably the most significant step in the history of aviation since the Wright brothers' machine staggered into the air, was the transition from the piston engine to the jet. The jet is a perfect example of someone building a better mousetrap. But why is it better? The piston engine had developed to a stage of great efficiency and reliability and was comparatively cheaper to manufacture. Jet engines require microscopic precision in engineering and use large quantities of rare and costly metals in their component parts. What prompted the airlines to sink fortunes into fleet renewals, scrapping relatively new airplanes in their scramble for the latest jet airplane?

It is fashionable today to detest anything military. Defense budgets come under fire from all sides, and yet it was supplying the military's needs that produced many of the comforts and conveniences the civilian world now regards as necessities. This is the case with the jet engine. The obvious military advantages of an airplane that could fly faster, higher, and farther, caused a quantum leap in engine design and development. You may argue that economy and cost considerations are low priorities for military hardware and the cost difference between piston and jet engines should have made the commercial transition a luxury few airlines could afford.

Well, the reason is simple: Jet airplanes are *more* economical in the long run than their piston-engined predecessors. The long-range economic advantage of flying more passengers greater distances at higher speeds equaled the considerable expenditure in equipment and crew utilization. The long-range gains far outweighed the short-range manufacturing costs.

Let us look for a while at the advantages of jet travel and why airline accountants wept for joy at the advent of the jet age.

Engines pull or push an airplane through the air. The more streamlined an airplane's shape, the less power it requires to overcome the forces resisting its smooth passage. The main forces of resistance are gravity and a devil known as "Drag."

We have learned to live with gravity and indeed could not survive comfortably without it. The greater power capability of a jet engine enables an airplane to overcome gravity at *a faster rate*. It can then attain higher altitudes more quickly and spend less time in the lower atmosphere where air is denser. Dense air provides more frictional resistance to movement. It is like wading through syrup instead of water.

As I mentioned earlier, smooth, efficient passage through the air depends upon a streamlined shape. You can throw a javelin faster and farther than a rock, even when they weigh the same. A propeller on a piston engine rotates through a diameter of anywhere between four and twenty feet. When those blades are spinning rapidly, they become, in effect, a solid metal disk that faces flat-on into the airflow. They literally tear up the smooth airflow into whirling eddies and currents of turbulent air, and the resultant friction is a major contribution to the total drag action upon the airplane. The maximum engine power cannot be utilized to perform its primary function of pushing or pulling the airplane through the air. Much of its power is lost in overcoming the drag that it creates itself by the propellers it drives. This combination of propeller and piston engine is, as we have seen, very inefficient.

The jet engine has, in most cases, no propeller to drive, and consequently can use more of its power output to move the airplane forward. Like the piston engine, it operates on a combustible mixture of fuel and air. The piston engine is unable to find sufficient air for a combustible mixture at high altitudes without the addition of boosters which use up much of the newly created power. The jet, by virtue of its greater power, can thrust through the thin upper atmosphere at high enough speeds to literally ram the available air into its engine, compressing it to a density suitable for combustion.

Exactly how does a jet engine work? The basic premise is extremely simple. Without resorting to drawings or blueprints, let me ask you to use your imagination to build a mental picture.

The firing cycle on a piston engine comprises induction, compression, ignition, and exhaust, all of which take place in a metal cylinder. In my days as a fledgling pilot, I remembered the firing cycle by memorizing the phrase, "suck, squeeze, bang, blow." The air and fuel mixture is drawn into the cylinder by the downstroke of the piston. It is compressed by the upstroke. Then a spark is fired into the compressed combustible mixture, creating a small explosion. Finally, gases are exhausted on the next downstroke.

53

In a jet engine, the cycle is similar, but the shape is different. The jet engine is a tube open at both ends. Air is rammed into the front end. A spinning fan called a compressor pumps the air under high pressure into the combustion chamber, where it is mixed with fuel (usually kerosene) and ignited by a constantly glowing plug. Air that has been compressed or heated has a powerful tendency to expand. The hot, expanding gases produced by the ignition of compressed air in the combustion chamber rush out through a nozzle at the rear of the engine. The backward force of the escaping gases results in an equal forward thrust to the airplane. Before they escape, the exhaust gases pass through the curved blades of a turbine. The resultant spinning motion of the turbine is translated by a shaft to the compressor that, originally, began the cycle.

What I have described is, of course, a very simple jet engine. Those mounted on your airplane are considerably more complex. They have up to sixteen sets of compressor fans up front and eight turbine fans at the rear. Much auxiliary equipment, such as electrical generators and cabin air compressors, is driven by the engines. Although a jet engine approximates the "suck, squeeze, bang, blow" of the old piston engine, it does it more effectively, due to the large amounts of air it can handle and without the metal-destroying action of pistons banging up and down several thousand times per minute. The internal works of a jet engine just hum away, spinning efficiently on the shaft. Because of the relatively few moving parts, metal wear is very small, thereby reducing maintenance and replacement considerably.

Not long ago, I came across an interesting use for these reliable, efficient machines that illustrates just how good they are. Over the past few years, Trans World Airlines has built a huge training and maintenance base just outside

Kansas City. The complex is as large as a fair-sized town and has commensurate power requirements. The TWA engineers took two outmoded jet engines left over from the earlier models of the Boeing 707 and mounted them permanently in a concrete blockhouse. They were then connected to large electrical generators and run alternately, to allow for regular maintenance on them without shutting down power. One engine, operating at half power, produces 17,000 kilowatts of electrical power. As this is well in excess of the needs of the complex, TWA sells the surplus power to the local power company. Those old engines have been running for more than two years without any mechanical failures. As you look out your window at those new improved engines on the wing, you may find this knowledge very reassuring. In all my years of commercial flying, I have personally experienced only one occasion when it became necessary to shut down a jet engine due to a mechanical failure or malfunction.

Before leaving the subject of engines, you might be interested to know how much fuel they consume. This varies with engine size and just how much of its power is being used at a given time.

Considering that there are more than twenty-five types of airliners flying today, it might be more useful if I gave you some averages. I will divide them into three categories. The largest are the jumbo jets, presently the Boeing 747, the Lockheed L-1011, and the Douglas DC-10. On take-off, their four engines gulp fuel at the rate of 150 gallons per minute. During cruise they consume a modest 56 gallons per minute. In the medium range of airplanes—the Boeing 707, Douglas DC-8, VC-10, and Convair 990—the take-off consumption is 100 gallons per minute, and 35 gallons per minute in cruise. The third category of airplanes, the three-engine Boeing 727 and the two-engine Douglas

DC-9, devour fuel at the rate of 75 gallons per minute on take-off and in cruise 27 gallons per minute.

If you take as an example an ordinary five-and-a-half-hour flight between New York and San Francisco by a 747, the pattern of fuel consumption is something like this: From take-off, through climbing, and up to the usual cruising altitude of approximately 33,000 feet, the 747 consumes 3,000 gallons, over a time span of 33 minutes. The plane increases its speed from 200 MPH at take-off to 300 MPH during climb, up to the cruising speed of 550 MPH. During cruise, the plane consumes over 80 percent of the total fuel for one flight. For the descent, from 33,000 feet to landing, only 500 gallons are eaten up. The average speed of the 18-minute descent is 480 MPH, which at the moment of landing has decreased to approximately 170 MPH. The total amount of fuel consumed in this flight is 20,000 gallons.

The fuel used for jet engines is low-grade kerosene (another plus in its favor). If you made a comparison with your family car, gallon for gallon, your fuel consumption on a coast-to-coast drive would be less than that required to get a Boeing 747 off the ground.

However, a 747 can carry almost four hundred passengers and only takes about six hours. In addition, it doesn't have to make all those annoying stops; it has its own washrooms on board!

The airplane's fuel is carried in tanks in the lower section of the fuselage and in the hollow wings. Some airplanes even carry fuel in the tail and rudder sections. Because of the vast fuel storage space available, we can fly from Los Angeles to London without making a single fuel stop.

Ecology groups occasionally contend that commercial airplanes contribute vast amounts of pollutants to the air.

In view of the large number of airplanes presently flying and their huge fuel consumption, such accusations may appear to be valid. Well, this is just not true. The fact is, that even at busy aviation centers such as New York and Chicago, jet airplanes contribute less than one percent to the total air pollution present in the atmosphere. Not content with this, the airlines are spending huge sums of money to clean up their engines and reduce this amount even more. (All my comments about pollution refer solely to jet airplanes, which have extremely clean burning engines. I know of no major U.S. air carrier that uses piston-engined aircraft on its routes.)

Now you might say, "But I flew on a propeller airplane just last week." The plane had propellers, yes, but it was almost certainly a "turbo-prop." This is an airplane powered by a basic jet engine that has a propeller attached to the front end of the jet's drive shaft. This type of engine is used on airplanes operated by smaller, second-level airlines such as those serving smaller towns and rural areas. Their main advantage is that they may used to replace outdated piston engines on otherwise airworthy airplanes with many years of useful service left in them.

At least half the turboprops flying today started life as piston-engine clunkers. The ugly duckling may not have turned into a beautiful swan, but it did grow into a pretty economical goose. The most common turboprops you will see in the United States are the Fairchild F-27 and the Convair 580; the first is a natural-born turboprop, and the latter, a sturdy hybrid.

By now you have acquired some basic understanding of how your airplane flies and, hopefully, are convinced that it is unlikely to fall from the sky, get lost, collide with another airplane, or pop you out of a window like a champagne cork, so you can relax and think about something else just as worrying.

The "something else" on everyone's mind these days is hijacking. Although the first hijacking occurred in Peru back in the thirties, it has only lately become a fad. I am intimately involved with the problem of hijacking, not only as an airline pilot, but also as the aircraft security specialist for the Air Line Pilots Association.

The subject of hijacking and flight security is enough to fill a book, one that I do not intend to write.* However, this book is about commercial aviation and would be incomplete without some mention of the hijacking phenomenon.

The most dramatic hijacking to date was the seizure and eventual destruction of four airplanes in the Middle East. These *political* hijackings constitute the most dangerous form of this crime. They are usually undertaken by a group of highly trained guerrillas, fanatically devoted to their cause. The combination of fanaticism and training makes them a highly volatile group to deal with.

Next on the list is the *extortion* hijacker or bomber. Unfortunately, he is often viewed as a folk hero. This dangerous criminal is no Robin Hood. He is a vicious, potential mass killer and must be treated as such.

Another category of hijackers is represented by the *fugitive*. Like the desperado of the Old West, he is fleeing across the border to escape justice for a previous crime.

---

* Several books have been written on the subject of hijacking, some of them obviously cashing in on recent dramatic occurrences, while others make a serious attempt to explain this frightening phenomenon. By and large I would say that almost all of them are either unreadable or grossly inaccurate. The only one worthy of mention was written by a working stewardess, Elizabeth Rich. Her book *Flying Scared* examines hijacking from the viewpoints of both the crew and the dispassionate, thorough researcher.

This man is usually a hardened criminal and a menace to society in the air or on the ground.

The most pitiful of the bunch is the *psychotic* hijacker. This individual is a living, walking 100 hundred percent failure. Beyond deciding to go to the bathroom when necessary, he is a quivering mass of indecision and fear. He will produce a thousand motives for his crime, each of them more bizarre than the last. Wherever he goes, he will be the same unwelcome, distasteful individual he was in his former home.

With some mighty prodding from the Air Line Pilots Association, the federal government and the airlines have abandoned their "let's-ignore-it-and-it-will-go-away" attitude. Sometimes, working together, sometimes at odds, the pilots, government, and the industry have undertaken massive security programs and research to combat this menace. International treaties exist for the provision of agreements on extradition or "no sanctuary" for hijackers, but unfortunately, very few nations have signed them. A major portion of the Air Line Pilots Association's antihijacking efforts is devoted to the attainment of a worldwide accord. It is a slow and sometimes frustrating business, but the occasional success we enjoy revives our hopes and encourages us to continue our battle.

What are your chances of being involved in such a dangerous situation? Airport security is now extremely effective. The hijacking curve plunged dramatically in the early part of 1973; every effort is being expended to ensure that the downward trend continues. Constant work and vigilance are paying off, and I hope that hijacking will soon become a past chapter in the history of commercial aviation. Your chances of becoming involved in an incident diminish daily.

To hasten the trend, you, as a passenger, can be of help.

Cooperate with your airlines in their security measures. You can keep your eyes and ears open when you travel. If you notice anything suspicious, report it immediately to your crew, or any airline employee. Believe me, they won't think you are being a nervous passenger; hijackings stopped being funny a long time ago.

At some point during the cruise portion of the flight the public address system crackles into life. "This is your captain speaking" are traditionally the first words but you may not be able to understand much else of what is said. The most persistently malfunctioning system on any airplane is the public address system from the cockpit. But maybe you don't care what the weather conditions are at your destination!

Airlines advise, encourage, and even plead with their pilots to make in-flight announcements. They say that the public relations gains are invaluable. Then, after all this fuss, they provide a system inferior to two cans and a piece of string.

During the 50 percent of the time that the system *is* working properly, passengers often have to sit through an embarrassing monologue, delivered in a dull monotone. Very few pilots deliver an informative, bright, and interesting announcement. The most common failing is overestimating the ability of the passengers to understand aeronautical jargon.

Some pilots go on forever, explaining in minute detail what is happening and what is about to happen. I recall one captain explaining over the PA system, "ATC is vectoring us for an ILS, because everyone is missing the ADF to four-right. Our ETA is now four-five." When a passenger asked her seat companion what it all meant, he grunted, "I guess he's practicing his alphabet."

On the other end of the scale, I know of another genuine announcement, which came after a long and tedious flight that had endured much turbulence and many delays. The captain picked up the PA mike and said, in staccato style, "This is the guy up front. The weather here is lousy. We're going back to Dayton."

One of the classics from the old propeller days was when a captain was forced to shut down one engine on a nighttime approach over the sea. Picking up the wrong mike, he unwittingly told New York air traffic control, "There's no need for concern. Even with one engine shut down, this bird will fly forever." He then informed the passengers, "We've got an emergency, request a direct vector to the airport. We got number-four engine shut down and this tub is flying like a housebrick."

Despite these handicaps, pilots do keep trying. Faulty PA systems are written up in the maintenance logbook, and there is a trend to try to improve pilot patter. Until this peak of perfection is reached, be patient and forgive the attempts at humor and lightheartedness. Once in a while a passenger will come across a pilot with a good sense of humor and a knowing delivery.

Once I was on a flight from New York to Las Vegas and our route took us close to the Grand Canyon. The captain obtained permission from air traffic control to go off his track for a few miles and descend to a lower altitude. As the airplane flew along the towering majesty of the Grand Canyon, the captain gave a wonderful dissertation on the beauty unfolding beneath us. I remember him finishing his announcement by saying: ". . . and as you know, the Grand Canyon was formed during the Ice Age. [Pause.] Of course, I don't remember it; but my wife does!"

Once on a Mohawk flight, as we climbed through the evening's murk, the PA clicked on and the pilot's voice announced: "As a replacement for the movie tonight, which we don't have, I would like to present to you, on behalf of myself, the crew, and the two thousand employees of Mohawk Airlines—on the left side of the airplane, ladies and gentlemen, the Sunset." That is the only PA announcement I have ever heard that drew a loud, spontaneous round of applause from the passengers.

From the point of view of airplane functions, the cruise portion of the flight is very uneventful. Very rarely does your speed or altitude vary and, as a passenger, your only diversions are the in-flight movies, if any, and the meal service.

On long flights, your meal is likely to be a leisurely affair: predinner drinks, entree, dessert, coffee, and liqueur afterward. On a short flight it is likely to be something quite different, especially if the airplane has a full passenger load. Having to prepare and serve meals to one hundred passengers in less than an hour and a half can be a pretty awesome task. Such an event is a regular occurrence while flying a short trip during the lunch or dinner hour. If you find yourself in such a situation, you can help yourself and the overworked stewardess by staying in your seat during the meal service. This leaves the aisles clear for the stewardesses and their carts. You can also help by keeping your requests for more coffee, extra drinks, etc., to a minimum.

On the subject of extra drinks, most airlines will not serve more than two drinks to each passenger on a flight of less than three hours. This does not include wine served with meals. As I explained earlier, the effects of alcohol are heightened by the increased cabin altitude in flight and your chances of becoming drunk are proportionately increased. Drunks, whatever their nature, are unwelcome almost everywhere, but especially on an airplane in flight. I have had a few run-ins with inebriated passengers during my career. Most of the incidents have been minor in their nature—obscene language and behavior, and on one occasion a passenger mistook the galley for the toilet. Many incidents have occurred because the passengers were nervous or apprehensive about the flight, and had a few belts before boarding to calm the nerves. It is my sincere hope that for such a nervous situation, this book will serve the same purpose!

Soon after the meal is finished and the stewardesses are cleaning up the debris of trays and glasses, the airplane takes a slight nose-down attitude. You hear a change in the engine noise. The cruise segment of the flight draws to a close. We are beginning the last phase of a routine flight: the descent.

7

Cleared to Land

The descent is carefully planned to bring the airplane to a low altitude (around 3,000 feet) at a slow speed (200 to 240 MPH), and into position for the start of its approach to the landing runway.

Most major airports have established a terminal control area to facilitate safe, efficient, and standardized handling of a large number of airplanes, all approaching the same point from different directions.

The descent is usually accomplished by bringing the airplane down in a series of steps. For example, you may descend from your cruise altitude of flight level 310 to flight level 240 and level off there for several minutes, and then be cleared by air traffic control down to the next lower altitude, and so on. These steps are usually necessary to accommodate other airplanes that have departed from your destination airport and are climbing to cruise level in your direction. They are climbing in a series of steps 2,000 or 3,000 feet beneath you, in the opposite direction. As a climbing airplane passes beneath and beyond you, it is cleared to climb to a higher altitude, and you are cleared to descend to a lower one. Pilots refer to this method of control as the "upside-down wedding cake."

Imagine a several-tiered wedding cake of gigantic proportions, turned upside down and placed, towering, over an airport. The different sized tiers, largest at the top, smallest at the bottom, represent the airspace limits of the airport's terminal control zone. The largest tier may be forty miles in diameter, the smallest, five.

When many airplanes arrive at a terminal control zone at the same time, they are directed by air traffic control into a circular flight pattern within a tier. Flying at regulated speeds and altitudes, airplanes enter in sequence behind other airplanes that arrived ahead of them. When sufficient space exists in the tier below, pilots are instructed, one at a time, to descend and join the merry-go-round in that layer.

The process of descending to each successive lower layer continues until you are in the lowest and smallest and in position for an approach to the landing runway. This system provides an excellent solution to a highly complex traffic problem. Due to the amount of air traffic and the separation that must be maintained between landing airplanes, utter chaos would result without this type of rigid control.

Delays and prolonged holding patterns do, of course, happen from time to time. The two major causes of holding delays are traffic saturation and poor weather conditions. The simultaneous arrival of fifty airplanes is obviously going to create a blockage in the bottom of the "cake."

Attempts have been made by the airlines to alleviate the problem. They try to schedule their arrivals at different times from their competitors. With only twenty-four hours a day and a phenomenal increase in the number of commercial flights, very little room remains for schedule maneuvering. At a number of major airports, available airport time has shrunk even further. Because of the noise caused by landing and departing airplanes, they now have a curfew, usually between 11:00 P.M. and 7:00 A.M. Their slack arrival periods are between 1:00 P.M. and 3:00 P.M., and

8:00 P.M. and 10:00 A.M. (local time). When planning his flight, your pilot will take time of arrival into account, and relying on his experience, he will have a pretty accurate idea of how much of a traffic delay the airplane will encounter.

The other, less predictable, cause of holding delays is bad weather. On a good day, officially referred to as CAVU (Clear and Visibility Unlimited), and unofficially as "gin-clear," pilots are able to see the airport and its runways from great distances. They are also able to see other airplanes around them and maintain a safe separation visually with help from the control tower. In good weather they are able to fly to the landing area at higher speeds, slowing at the last minute for the final approach and landing. This reduces or eliminates holding delays at higher altitudes.

Bad weather, on the other hand, can effectively congest the final "cake layer" and prevent any traffic flow at all. To understand the extent of this problem, we must first determine what commercial pilots would consider bad weather.

Modern jets are large, heavy, stable machines and during the approach and landing they are able to shrug off the major effects of turbulent air. Rain and ice can be swept aside by very efficient built-in rain-removal and deicing systems. For moderate rain the pilot relies on a sturdier version of the windshield wipers found on automobiles. During a landing in a very heavy downpour, the pilot only has to press a button to spread a rain-repellent fluid across his windshield that causes the raindrops to break up and fly off the surface of the glass immediately on contact. The results are remarkable. It is rather like suddenly having a clear picture appear on a fuzzy television screen. The watery darkness of the windshield is suddenly replaced by a clear view of the landing area.

67

Icing, the dread of pilots in the old piston days, is no more than a minor irritation on a modern jet. When icing conditions exist in freezing clouds or rain, thick layers of ice accumulate on the wings, control surfaces, and engine intakes. Besides the hazard of extra weight created by the accumulation of ice, it can radically alter the shape of the wing, thereby reducing its lift. A large enough ice accumulation can also choke off the airflow into the engines. These problems are alleviated by tapping very hot air from the compressor section of the engines and running it through hundreds of yards of pipes located just beneath the airplane's skin where ice accumulates. The heat from these pipes is sufficient to warm the airplane's skin and prevent any ice from forming.

What, then, is bad weather? Wind, ice, and rain are effectively dismissed from that category. About the only thing you have left is visibility, or more accurately, the lack of it. For the purpose of this discussion we can assume that a pilot must be able to see the runway to set his airplane down on it. His airplane can weigh hundreds of tons and can be traveling at speeds of up to 160 MPH. If he is landing in visibility conditions of half a mile, he has less than three seconds between catching his first glimpse of the runway and making several decisions. He must evaluate his position in relation to the runway and either decide to continue the landing or climb out and perform a "missed approach." He may then decide to go to another airport that has better weather conditions, or he may decide that sufficient fuel remains to hold for another hour, after which he will attempt one more approach and landing. His crew is continuously monitoring the weather situation at the destination airport and possible alternate airports, in case such a diversion should become necessary. In addition, by law, he must have sufficient fuel remaining when he lands or misses the landing to climb out and fly to a suitable alternate airport and perform an approach and landing there.

Many people equate "missed approaches" with "aborted landings," but they are two different operations. A missed approach occurs when, at some time on the approach prior to the actual landing, the pilot decides not to continue and climbs his airplane out of the approach path to either try again or divert to another airport. An aborted landing, on the other hand, is very rare. This occurs just before the point of touchdown, should the pilot suddenly find an obstruction on the runway, maybe a truck or another airplane. The only aborted landings I have ever performed have been in training situations.

If you suffer from sinus problems or have a head cold, it is during descent that you are most likely to suffer some discomfort. During the time you have been in cruise, the air in your ears and sinus cavities has adjusted to the lower, less dense air pressure in the cabin. At the same time, due to the constant renewal of air-conditioned air, the mucous membranes have become very dry. As the airplane descends, it enters much denser and therefore higher-pressure air. The more rapid the descent, the more rapid the pressure change.

A head cold has the effect of swelling the membrane in your ear canals. Your sinuses and this swelling can close off entire sections of the ear canals and sinuses. As you descend, the higher-pressure atmosphere you are entering tries to force its way through the sinuses and ear passages to balance the pressure. It is unable to do so when these passages are blocked, and the resulting imbalance of pressure can cause severe discomfort.

There are a few ways to alleviate this problem. The most obvious is not to fly when you have a head cold. If that is impractical, or if you suffer from a chronic sinus condition, medication may be taken to relieve your discomfort.

Fairly constant use of one of the many decongestant nasal sprays, such as Neosynephrin, will help in mild cases and for short periods of time. A commercial preparation called Sinutab not only works on the sinuses, but also has some beneficial effects on the ears. The effects last for about four hours. If you are planning a long flight of more than four hours, ask your doctor to prescribe a more powerful nasal spray called Afrin. The effects of this preparation will last for a full twelve hours.

To combat the effects of the very dry atmosphere, take along a nasal spray container filled with clean water. An occasional spray into each nostril will keep the nasal passages moist and open.

With all these preparations, remember that beneficial effects will become apparent only about thirty minutes after taking them.

If you have no medication with you, or prefer not to take any, it will help you clear your sinuses and ears if you perform the exercise known as Valsalva's method. This simply requires that you take a deep breath, hold your nose closed, close your mouth, and try to exhale as hard as you can. This may hurt a little, but it usually forces the pressure to equalize. You may have to repeat this exercise several times during the descent.

The pressure-change problem can be quite painful and very frightening to babies and small children, for they have neither the understanding nor the capability to cope with it. If you intend to travel with children, I strongly recommend that you change your plans if they are suffering from head colds, or at least get your doctor's advice.

If you have taken none of these precautions before the descent and suffer from sinus problems you may experience some degree of pain and even temporary partial deafness. Although the effects will probably disappear within a few hours after landing, they might cause an infection in your sinuses or middle ear.

As the descent phase starts, the FASTEN SEAT BELT sign goes on. We are reentering the region where we are most likely to encounter cloud turbulence. The stewardesses complete their cleaning-up tasks and an air of quiet settles about the cabin. In the cockpit, your crew is going through the pilot's litany, reading checklists to doubly ensure that all necessary tasks have been performed to prepare their craft for landing. If the approach is by means of instruments, because of bad weather, the atmosphere in the cockpit is particularly tense. Each crew member, much like an athlete before a maximum attempt, will prime himself in preparation for the approach and landing. A sharpening of one's mental and physical reactions replaces the more relaxed atmosphere that existed during cruise.

There are two main types of instrument approaches used throughout the world. One of them, GCA (Ground Control Approach), is used almost exclusively at military airfields, and only occasionally by commercial airlines.

A controller in a radar installation monitors a split radar screen in front of him. In the top half of the screen is etched a side view of the "glide slope" (an imaginary line of descent to a touchdown point). On the bottom half is etched the "glide path" (a bird's eye view of the descent path the airplane must follow).

As an airplane gets within radar range, it is seen by the controller as a blip on both halves of the screen. By voice control, he tells the pilot to fly up or down (according to the glide slope), and left or right (according to the glide path). The airplane must stay on the line of descent and within boundaries in order to land correctly. By following the controller's directions, a pilot is able to maintain a steady descent to the touchdown point while remaining perfectly aligned with the runway.

GCA controllers are a breed apart. Their dedication and awesome responsibility is legend among pilots. As a military pilot I, for one, owed my life to them on at least two occasions. From a personal viewpoint, I regret their general disappearance from the commercial aviation scene.

To replace these fine technicians, at commercial airports a device known as Instrument Landing System (ILS) has been perfected. This is the most common instrument approach aid in the world. It consists of two basic components: a transmitter located on the ground at the airport, and a receiver installed in the airplane. The transmitter sends out two very narrow radio beams. The first beam points from the ground up the glide slope the airplane must descend upon. The second is transmitted horizontally as a narrow fan along which the airplane must fly to align with the runway. These signals are received by the airplane's receiver, which converts them into a visual display for the pilots. Two sensitive needles, one for the glide slope, and one for the glide path, show the pilot any deviation above or below the glide slope, or any wandering to the left or right of the glide path. When the needles are perfectly aligned, the airplane is flying down an extremely narrow radio beam, to the point of landing. Flying this instrument is like trying to precisely line up two very sensitive cross hairs, exactly in the center of a circle. Accurate adherence to this instrument will place an airplane in an almost perfect position and attitude for landing.

I said earlier that a pilot must be able to see the runway in order to land. This is not strictly true. The continuing development of the ILS, and increased sensitivity of autopilots, is now making totally blind, fully automatic landings a reality.

The autopilot (they call it "George" in old war movies), has the basic capability of holding an airplane in a selected attitude. By means of a series of gyroscopes and associated hydraulic impulses, it can fly an airplane straight and level, in a turn, or climbing and descending. Its present stage of development now permits it to fly along a radio beam. It does this by moving the airplane controls so that it will fly exactly down a glide slope and glide path. In addition the autopilot also adjusts engine power to achieve the precise required speed for any type of approach.

More recent autopilot models, combined with the new ultrasensitive ILS, will not only fly the approach but will automatically reduce the throttle at the instant of touchdown and actually perform a passable landing without any assistance from the pilot.

I have been asked hundreds of times if these technological advances are the death knell for my profession. I am reminded of a story I heard in a nightclub a few years ago. An airplane had just taken off, and as the passengers settled down, the public address system clicked on and a recorded voice said: "Good evening, ladies and gentlemen, may I welcome you aboard flight 480, the very first fully automated commercial flight in aviation history. There is no flight crew on board this airplane; they have been replaced by a highly sophisticated computerized autopilot. Please relax and enjoy the flight, with the assurance that nothing can go wrong—go wrong—go wrong—go wrong. . . ."

Although mildly amusing, the story points out that in certain situations men cannot be replaced by a machine. The variables inherent in flying require the evaluation of an experienced human being who can take instantaneous action. The wonderful machines and devices now available to a pilot are there to assist him and act as an extension of his skill and capabilities, not to replace him. After all, doesn't the U.S.S. *Enterprise* in "Star Trek" need Captain Kirk?

For the passenger, the first indication of an impending approach is a small whirring sound accompanied by a slight shuddering of the airplane. If you have a strategically located window seat, you may notice the flaps sliding into place and extending into the airflow past the wings. If you are an inexperienced air traveler, the next sound you hear will probably increase your pulse rate a few beats. There is a sudden, loud, shuddering *thump* and the sound of rushing air. A good cabin crew will prepare you for this by making an anticipatory announcement that "the loud sound you will soon hear is the sound of our landing gear being lowered and locked into place." More whirring noises are heard as the remainder of the flaps are extended. Then, the engines' whine builds and fades as the pilot makes power adjustments to remain "on the beam" at the correct speed. Looking down from the window, you may catch occasional glimpses of the ground through the breaks in the cloud. The next thing you see is concrete rushing by a few feet below you. A small silence, as all the power is reduced, and (hopefully) a small jar, as the main landing wheels kiss the runway.

The nose wheel is lowered onto the runway, and as the brakes are applied, you feel yourself leaning forward in your seat as your own momentum lags behind the airplane's deceleration. With a tremendous roar, the engines' power momentarily increases. The jet outlets at the rear of each engine are closed off. Simultaneously, forward-facing louvers around the sides of the engines spring open, to direct the jets' thrust forward, slowing the momentum of the airplane even more.

After a few seconds, the engines' noise dies as their "thrust" position is switched from "reverse" to "normal." With the engines at idling speed, the airplane turns off the runway. It must clear to allow the other planes hot on your heels to land.

Moving from the exitway, or "high-speed turnoff," and onto the taxiway, the pilot switches radio frequencies to ground control and requests taxi clearance to the terminal. A staccato burst of instructions and we are on our way in. Having performed their task of reducing the approach and landing speed, and shortening the landing roll, the flaps are retracted into the wings. The engines' noise diminishes slightly as one of them is shut down. Most airlines, no matter what type of airplane, follow this "one-engine-out" taxi procedure, to save both fuel and wear on the engine. The amounts saved appear to be negligible, but multiply those small savings by a couple of hundred airplanes performing several landings each day and the results run into thousands of dollars.

Like the taxi out at your originating airport, the taxi in may take several minutes. As it commences, the public address system clicks into life and your stewardess welcomes you to your destination. If she is really on the ball, she will also inform you of the outside temperature and the local time.

When she has finished telling you how nice it has been serving you, she will request that you remain seated until the airplane has come to a complete stop at the gate.

Apart from highway speed limits, this is undoubtedly the most ignored instruction in the world. I don't know why it is, but I will guarantee that 75 percent of your fellow passengers will immediately leap to their feet, pulling their coats from the overhead rack, usually draping them over the heads of anyone sitting in front of them. Bending their bodies like pretzels, they struggle into their outer garments and then start edging their way down the aisle toward what they have decided will be the exit.

The urge to get off the plane as quickly as possible, once the airplane has turned off the runway, is understandable. You can't believe you made it in one piece, can you? But this lemminglike rush is not only discourteous to other passengers, but dangerous as well. I once had a passenger badly gored by an umbrella being carried by an overladen lady who was standing in the aisle when I found it necessary to make an abrupt stop. The damage awarded at the subsequent court case was a costly cure for her impatience.

Apart from the danger to yourself and your fellow passengers, such a rush rarely achieves anything. With the exception of those times when you are traveling without any checked baggage, you can be first off the airplane, and first at the baggage collection point—but you will still be there when the last deplaning passenger strolls up. Chances are you will have to wait until everyone else has departed—inevitably the last piece of baggage to appear belongs to the passenger in the greatest hurry.

In addition, if your landing airport happens to be one of the busier terminals, such as Kennedy, in New York, O'Hare, in Chicago, or Los Angeles, you are likely to be caught in the most frustrating trap of all—the gate delay.

At all airline terminals, each airline is allocated a certain number of gates for boarding and disembarkation. During the busy hours (9:00 A.M. to 1:00 P.M. and 5:00 P.M. to 8:00 P.M.), if one of the departing flights is delayed for some reason, an incoming flight allocated that same gate will usually have to wait for it to be vacated. These delays can run from a few minutes up to an hour. If you are jammed in the aisle, laden with your belongings, an already trying situation can turn into a nightmare of embarrassment and discomfort.

Instead, I recommend that you comfortably remain in your seat until the doors are open and deplaning begins. You will step into the terminal, relaxed and unhurried, better prepared to adjust yourself to a three-dimensional world again.

8

Your Pilot: Man or Superman?

A sudden flash of lightning illuminates the cabin, high-lighting the pale, sweating faces of the passengers. Panic begins to break through their thin veneer of calm as the airplane lurches violently in the storm's turbulence. The glow from the fire in the number-two engine grows brighter, as the flames feed on the spreading film of gasoline from the broken fuel line.

In the eerie glow of the cockpit you can just make out strong, tanned hands grasping the control yoke and a determined mouth issuing cool, clipped commands.

Another violent lurch, and warning lights flash on the instrument panel as another engine quits. Just as all seems lost, the clouds thin and through the ghostly fog appears the fuzzy brightness of the landing lights, pointing the way to the landing runway. Pulling back on the control yoke to break the airplane's earthward plunge, the captain cuts the throttles on the two remaining engines and the wheels meet the runway's surface.

Letting his face relax into attractive but tired lines, Charlton Heston casually remarks to the crew, "I think I could use a cup of coffee."

Even in this age of "realism" in the cinema you will never see a pilot portrayed as anything but the Hollywood image: the handsome, cool, superman hero. If Charlton

Heston or John Wayne were just starting in movies today, they could carve out an entire career portraying airline captains. In Hollywood's cockpits there are no "uglies" or antiheroes.

Until the midsixties, movie heroes, whether they were cops, private eyes, cowboys, soldiers, or airline pilots, were always clean-cut, manly, and handsome. When directors and producers began to make their art imitate life, the typecasting of leading men undertook a sudden metamorphosis and the heroes were suddenly not uniformly handsome. They swore and drank a great deal, and some of them even lived with their leading ladies without benefit of clergy. All the heroes, that is, with the exception of the pilot, whose former characterization was maintained in the face of "tell-it-like-it-is" cinematography.

Why did this image persist? In real life airline pilots look remarkably like anybody else. They are fat, thin, tall, or short. Most are of average looks, a few are downright ugly, and even fewer are handsome. (Still fewer, at the time of this writing, are *women*.)

I suppose that the gold braid, flashing wings, and rakish hat may tend to divert attention from the potbellies, false teeth, and balding heads that some pilots have. I also think that the traveling public desperately wants to believe in the demigod image of the airline pilot. Deep down in all of us is a very understandable reluctance to place our lives in the hands of a complete stranger and mere mortal, as he takes us into an alien and unnatural environment.

I would be less than human were I not pleased with the flattering image I share with my fellow pilots, but holding that determined look does make my facial muscles ache, and my pants tend to sag when I suck my stomach in!

Contrary to popular belief, pilots are made and not born. Attaining fairly high levels of physical fitness, education, intelligence, and coordination are the necessary

80

prerequisites for this exciting and rewarding career. The days of the ragged, barefoot boy hanging around country airports and washing down airplanes and pumping gas for the privilege of being near his gods and getting an occasional hour of wondrous free flight instruction is long past. The cockpit of a modern jet airliner, overflowing with advanced electronics equipment, is not the place for romanticism. What, then, makes a pilot, and where does he or she come from?

More than 75 percent of today's airline pilots started their flying careers in the military. War not only speeded the rapid development of airplanes, but also provided the men to fly them. For instance, literally thousands of potential store clerks, doctors, dentists, cabdrivers, and beach bums became highly skilled flyers because of World War II. Today they form the nucleus of the airline industry. The remaining 25 percent came to their careers without the benefit of free military flight training. They learned their profession by paying for it themselves and graduating from private light airplane schools.

Whatever a pilot's beginnings, after enduring the rigors of an airline training school, he or she emerges as a true airline professional. Perhaps a brief look at the training they undergo will give you more confidence in these men and women who fly the big jets.

The hiring requirements for pilots vary from airline to airline but more often depend upon the system of supply and demand. When pilot jobs are scarce, the employment requirements are extremely high. Then the airlines are able to select only those pilots with the most flight experience. Usually, the more experience a pilot has prior to airline training the greater guarantee of success in passing the training. This lower failure rate saves thousands of dollars in training costs.

During periods of rapid expansion, the airlines actively

solicit pilot applicants to fill their requirements, and consequently have to lower their employment standards. I do not mean that they will hire just anybody. Even when at a minimum, employment standards are extremely high in comparison with other professions. On the average, to be employed by an airline one must have excellent physical and mental capabilities, be a college graduate, possess an instrument flight and commercial flying license, be under the age of thirty, and have about 1,000 hours of flying experience.

After being classroom tested by instructors, prodded and poked by doctors, examined and interviewed by a board of hard-nosed senior captains, a candidate may be selected for employment. When selecting a pilot, the airline bears in mind that one day he will be in complete charge of up to $25 million of their equipment, and several hundred passengers. It's not surprising that they check the candidates carefully!

On the day a new pilot reports for training, he is given his magic number, his position on the company's seniority list. No other number will have the importance that his seniority number has. This number places him on the ladder of his career. It will determine throughout his career where he will be stationed, what flights and types of airplanes he may fly, when he gets promoted, and how much salary he will make. His seniority number is not transferable to another airline. If a pilot quits one airline and joins another, he must start at the very bottom of the seniority list of the new airline. This is why pilots rarely move around from airline to airline. In fact, fewer than one percent of airline pilots ever resign their positions.

The next three or four weeks are spent in the classroom, learning the construction and operating instructions for every type of airplane he might be assigned to. After eight hours in a classroom, he will need at least four more hours of private study each day.

Pilots usually share an apartment with two or three classmates who provide companionship, spread the living costs, and act as trial examiners. I can recall the system I devised with my roommates; as one of us was performing some chore, such as cooking, dishwashing, driving to school, etc., the other would fire questions at him from a stack of flash cards.

Airline training centers are inhabited by young men who wander from classroom to classroom toting fifty-pound "brain bags" crammed with homework, muttering numbers, temperatures, watts, and voltages to themselves. These students are easily distinguishable from the instructors by their haggard, worried expressions.

In addition to understanding the mechanics of the airplane, a trainee must also learn air navigation, flying procedures, and radio work. As one of my roommates remarked prior to the examinations, "Not only can I build the airplane with a pair of tin shears and a hammer, I can also construct a bloody box to put it in!"

After successfully completing the final ground school examination, trainee-pilots edge a little closer to actually flying: They begin the "simulator" phase of training. The simulator, or "sweat box" as it is commonly known, is an electronic marvel. Because commercial jet airplanes are very costly to operate they are not used for all training flights. Also, the number of emergency procedures that must be learned and practiced by a trainee makes the airplane likely to be damaged, or even lost. The simulator eliminates these problems. What, then, is a simulator?

If you slice off the cockpit of an airplane, and mount it on hydraulic legs to provide pitch-and-roll movement, add recorded engine noise regulated by movement of the throttle, install closed circuit TV to simulate outside landscape, and connect it to a huge computer that can produce any emergency situation imaginable, you will have some idea of what a simulator is. It feels and responds exactly like a real airplane and most pilots will tell you that a few minutes after commencing a training session, they completely forget that they are flying a simulator. The pilot can encounter every type of in-flight emergency, even "crash" it. Pushing a few buttons and flicking a few switches will restore it to a perfect flying machine. He can fly "sunny-day" visual approaches to an airport, or fight his way through thick fog or turbulent thunderstorms. It is here that he learns his trade.

After six to ten two-hour periods, where the pilot copes with clanging warning bells, flashing warning lights, engine fires and failures, electrical blackouts, hydraulic failures, explosive decompressions, and any other diabolical combinations the instructor can devise, he may be judged ready for a "practical simulator check-ride" from an inspector of the Federal Aviation Administration. By the time you have realized that he is not the snarling hatchet man everyone fears him to be, you have probably successfully passed your check-ride.

At last comes that magic, nervous day when the pilot climbs aboard a real airplane to begin the final phase of training. He undergoes three to six two-hour training flights where he practices his newly acquired emergency skills and learns the routine as well as the pleasurable tasks of his job. When the flight instructor feels the pilot is ready, he will be scheduled for yet another check-ride from the Federal Aviation Administration, this time on a real plane.

During such a check-ride, the pilot will be required to demonstrate his skills and knowledge in handling both normal take-offs and engine failures on take-off, standard instrument departures, and recovery from "stall" (when the airplane loses sufficient flying speed, and "drops" from the sky). Returning to the airport, the pilot will perform several instrument approaches and landings, some with one or two engines shut down and some without using flaps. In a single two-hour check-ride, a pilot will cope with more emergency situations than he is likely to encounter during thirty years of airline flying. When that FAA inspector signs the pilot's license, indicating proficiency on that particular type of airplane, it is one of the proudest and most relieved moments in a pilot's life. He then rushes anxiously back to the training center to find out where he is being assigned. On my airline, for instance, you could be sent to New York, Chicago, Kansas City, Los Angeles, or San Francisco. Twenty-four hours later, with a hangover from the celebration party, the pilot is on his way to a new home and a new career.

After one scheduled flight, or "line-check," with a supervisory pilot, he becomes a probationary pilot. He remains one for a year, polishing and honing his skills and trying to live on the $6,000 to $9,000 earned during that period. At the end of this period, three important things happen. The pilot is no longer subject to arbitrary dismissal, he feels a great sense of pride and accomplishment, and his salary jumps about 120 percent!

In the cockpit a pilot's normal progression starts with a period as flight engineer. During this time, he does not have an opportunity to fly the airplane. Instead, he is responsible for the in-flight mechanical functioning of all the airplane's systems. This is undoubtedly the most frustrating job a pilot can have. However, time has a way of changing most things, and soon he is promoted to first officer (copilot).

On most airlines, the first officer has the responsibility of assisting the captain in flying the airplane, planning the flight, and performing the navigation. Some airlines have an additional position, usually on very long flights, which is assigned to a second officer. His tasks are primarily to relieve the other crew members during their rest periods; the rest of the time he sits behind the captain, checking his haircut, laughing at his jokes, and dreaming of the day he, too, will wear those four stripes on his sleeves.

Finally, we arrive at the ultimate position: the captain. To attain this lofty position, a pilot must serve in all the others for a number of years. He must then go back to the training center and endure even more intense training than the initial training I have described already. Next, he goes through several months of continuous line-checks, and a semifinal and final line-check with a hard-nosed supervisory captain.

I remember that when I had finished my upgrading, I asked the supervisor who had given me my "final ride" what yardstick he used for making his "thumbs-up-or-thumbs-down" decision. He answered, "I ask myself, would I put my wife and kids on this man's airplane if he were the captain?"

I have been a pilot for more than half my life, first flying fighter airplanes in the Royal Air Force and the Royal Australian Air Force, then as a bush pilot in the Australian outback, and ultimately as an airline pilot.

The fighter pilots I flew with displayed a strong aggressiveness, which they needed to perform their specific tasks as well as to stay alive in a combat environment. The pilots I encountered in the bush had toughness and inventiveness as their major suit. In airline flying, those same pilots displayed precision and professionalism. In summary, a pilot for hire develops a chameleonlike ability to emphasize or repress certain attributes or shortcomings according to the varying job requirements.

All pilots are egotists and are proud of their skills. They will demonstrate them at the drop of a hat—especially to fellow pilots. The fighter pilot displays his particular skills by his aggressiveness and kill rate, the end product of his job. The bush pilot, flying in an adventurous and dangerous environment, demonstrates his skill by simply surviving.

None of those attributes is required when flying large, expensive airplanes containing paying passengers. The airline pilot's *only* outlet for demonstrating his capabilities is in the *precision* of his flying. Almost all of the airline pilots I know fly every trip as though the fate of the world hinged on their ability to keep their airplanes at the exact required altitude, speed, and direction at all times. When he flies at 30,000 feet, it must be 30,000 feet; 29,050, or 30,050 feet, are just not good enough, not for a "professional"!

From time to time I have tested this widespread obsession among airline pilots for absolute precision. For a short time I have flown just off altitude—within acceptable limits but not exactly "on target." The other pilots in the crew, if they were junior to me, become politely perturbed, as though that fifty-foot difference were a personal affront. Older senior pilots would quickly point out the transgression in no uncertain terms. As a passenger, I'm sure you appreciate this obsession for precision. For a pilot, it is the symbol of his craft.

Aspersions and doubts may be cast upon the ancestry, legitimacy, and even honesty of pilots, but never their professionalism. As a group they wrap it around themselves like the American flag and defy anyone to shoot them through it. Once, during a long flight, in a moment of idle reflection, I suggested to a very senior captain that we are, in fact, "artisans." After all, I mused, we do practice our skills in a mechanical environment and are paid salaries for specific work performed. It took several cups of coffee and the aid of two stewardesses before his temper and blood pressure had lowered to the point where he could speak clearly once more.

As I advanced in years and experience, I came to appreciate his views. I can no longer classify airline flying as a job; it has become a way of life. If this were not true, why, then, would so many pilots give so much of their time assisting in the advancement of commercial aviation?

In the United States most commercial pilots belong to an organization called the Air Line Pilots Association, or ALPA.° It is a large organization with more than 40,000 members and concerns itself with every facet of commercial aviation from the design of airports to the installation of new types of passenger seats. It has a number of full-time staff, but its main work force is drawn from the ranks of working pilots. Hundreds of men and women devote themselves to jobs that hold little recognition and even less pay. For them, flying a plane is more than just a job.

ALPA has another side less noble in purpose, though requiring the same degree of devotion from its workers. It is also a labor organization (pilots dislike the term union). It negotiates contracts for its membership and presents a united front on various issues crucial to the airlines, the pilots, and the public. ALPA is, in fact, a unique example of elite unionization.

So far, I have described how a pilot is made, but what of the person? What kind of man selects a career that can be cut off on four separate occasions each year? Every six

° The pilots of American Airlines have their own organization, the Allied Pilots Association.

months, no matter how long he has been flying, a pilot must pass an FAA check-flight. Every six months, he must also pass a government medical examination. Failure in either test means his flying days are over.

Why does he do it?

Ambition is crucial to almost all fields of human endeavor. The desire to be the boss, the overseer, the foreman, or the captain produces superior products and services in our society. The status attached to high position is probably at least as great a motivating force as the financial rewards it carries. Large corporations have long recognized this urge for status and have responded by substituting important-sounding titles for salary increases to ambitious young employees. As a result, some corporations have more vice-presidents than a hound dog has fleas. The status attached to the job of an airline captain is, however, more significant. His position is not just titular: He must have proven his capabilities to obtain the position and then reprove them for the rest of his career.

Money is also a motivating factor in selecting a career. Just how great a motivation is money for a pilot, or to put it another way, how much does he make? I know of no other profession that evokes such widespread envy and exaggeration as the flying profession. Every reference to an airline pilot in a newspaper or magazine always refers to him as a "$60,000-a-year-pilot." It is almost an accusation, and has taken on the same meaning as the policeman's "alleged perpetrator."

I can recall some contract negotiations a few years ago that illustrate what the general public thinks of our way of life. After months of fruitless bargaining, the management- and pilot-negotiating teams had reached an impasse. About thirty proposals from the pilots remained unresolved and the unpleasant prospect of a strike loomed closer. The leader of the pilots' negotiating committee stunned everyone in the conference room by stating: "It seems the only way to get these negotiations off dead center is for the pilots to reduce their demands. Therefore, I wish to negotiate only three items with you." He continued in the shocked silence that followed this extraordinary statement: "One, we wish to make as much money as our brothers-in-law think we make; two, we want as much time off as our neighbors think we get; and three, we want to go to bed with as many stewardesses as our wives think we do." Then he added: "And we want the last demand to be retroactive to June of last year!"

I don't know how much effect this had on the final agreement but I do know that it gave all concerned a hearty laugh, and pointed out some exaggerated ideas the general public has of our employment benefits.

The length of an airline pilot's career is fixed by the federal government. If he successfully passes the multitude of physical and practical tests and examinations he must undergo, he will have to hang up his wings at the age of sixty. This gives him approximately thirty years to make himself and his family financially secure.

As I pointed out earlier in this chapter, he spends the first year of his career balancing on the thin edge of poverty while trying to provide for himself and his family on the $6,000 to $9,000 per year he will make. By today's standards, that could hardly be considered a princely sum.

When a pilot escapes from the probationary-pilot classification, he takes a gratifying leap in salary. After this, his salary will depend upon accumulated years of service, rank, the type of airplane he flies, his duties, and the number of hours he actually flies per month. Generally speaking, the bigger the airplane, the higher the pay. The kind of plane he flies is determined by seniority. The number of hours he flies is fixed by contractual agreement. It varies from airline to airline but generally is about seventy-five hours each month. This does not mean that he will fly seventy-five hours; once again, his seniority will determine his access to the available flying hours. The greater his seniority, the more chance he has of flying a full month of seventy-five hours.

Starting as a junior engineer on a "junior" airplane (usually the smallest in the airline's fleet), he will make approximately $16,000 a year. A junior first officer, subject to the same seniority limitation, can expect to earn approximately $19,000 a year. A junior captain starts to break into higher brackets with an average annual salary of $32,000. From this point on, the financial future begins to look very rosy. With increasing seniority, rank, and upgrading to flying bigger and better-paying airplanes, a pilot will progress at irregular intervals to the point of earning $65,000 per year—if he is fortunate enough to fly for an airline that owns jumbo jets. A rough calculation shows that over a thirty-year career, a pilot's total earnings would average $34,000 a year. It is true that some airline pilots are very wealthy, but this is due to inherited wealth or income other than from the airlines.

"Getting as much time off as our neighbors think we get" is perhaps the least-exaggerated facet of our image. The amount of time a pilot may legally fly is controlled by government regulation but maximum time negotiated in contractual agreements is usually much less and, as I mentioned earlier, will usually be around seventy-five hours. Those seventy-five hours are not calculated only on actual flying time but include on-duty time, which reduces actual flying time to sixty-five hours. With allowance for a calculated ratio for time-away-from-home, a pilot may fly sixty-five hours but accumulate seventy-five hours of pay. Depending upon whether he is flying international or domestic, he will work between ten and fifteen days each month. Although that sounds very attractive (and indeed it is), some portion of his days off will be spent studying flight manuals, taking physicals, and training and performing general administrative duties allied to his job. If you are making a comparison with someone who works a five-day week, twenty-day month, remember that when a pilot is away from home for ten to fifteen days, he doesn't get home each evening.

Paradoxically, it is the junior pilot who usually gets the most time off because he has insufficient seniority to fly a maximum number of flights each month. Instead, he spends much of his time hanging around his home waiting to be called as a reserve pilot. On the other hand, he is guaranteed a "minimum wage" equivalent to sixty-four hours of flying time per month, whether he flies them or not.

What do pilots do on their days off? Well, if you scratch an airline pilot, you often find a businessman underneath. Thanks to the free time they have, and a salary that provides them with investment capital, it is very common for them to go into all kinds of businesses. They range from dry-cleaning establishments to the breeding of thoroughbred horses. Many of these enterprises are designed to legally provide some degree of relief from the clutching hands of the Internal Revenue Service; others are hobbies; and some are intended as serious, large-scale business enterprises. One pilot I know discovered the secret of making intricate puzzle rings and jewelry while on loan to an airline in the Middle East. He supplemented his income by manufacturing and selling these rings for many years. Now in retirement, he has a thriving, profitable, and full-time business that not only occupies his time but meets his financial needs.

Not all pilots spend their free time in pursuit of profit. Many are very active in the affairs of their communities. One young pilot is also mayor of the midwestern town in which he lives. Many others involve themselves actively in political enterprises, and a few have successfully run for Congress and the Senate.

Private flying, golf, sailing, and other sports also occupy the spare time of many others, while some just goof off. I even know one who writes books!

Now that I've explained salary and seniority, all that remains is sex. The public image of the steely-eyed demigod at the controls of an airplane includes the lustful, insatiable international stud. At cocktail parties and other social functions usually half the men present give me a sly dig in the ribs and a knowing leer when they hear what my profession is. A modest little smile and a shrug of the shoulders is all that is necessary to sustain this virile image that most men seem to enjoy. I confess to making such mute comment on occasion, reasoning that everyone needs to be admired whether it be justified or not. Bearing that in mind and knowing that my wife will read this book, I'm finding this the most difficult part to write. In the interests of honesty it is best to give you the facts as I know them. Certainly, part of the image is justified. Pilots live in close contact with many young and pretty women and flash their way through some of the most exotic cities in the world. I have, however, seen more extramarital relationships among the employees of an average business office than among pilots. It is true that a number of pilots have a deserved reputation as rakes but those individuals would be the same whatever their occupation.

Stories of wild crew orgies abound in the industry. Most of them are the result of wishful thinking or gross exaggerations. All, however, cannot be dismissed, for airline pilots, despite their high-altitude environment, are not angels. There is a true, confirmed story of a Nordic crew on a layover at a hotel in Lisbon. They started a party one afternoon in one of the rooms. It must have gotten very warm as the party progressed, for one of the stewardesses, a beautiful woman, stripped to her dusting powder prior to lapsing into unconsciousness. This collapse, I believe, was brought on by fatigue from lifting a large number of heavy glasses. The rest of the crew decided that the ancient Viking ceremony of burial was in order. This was not unreasonable, considering the young lady's deathlike trance. Removing the room door from its hinges, they placed the naked woman on the door and, carrying it high above their heads, descended down the grand staircase to the main lobby of the hotel. They arrived at the height of the pre-dinner rush, chanting valedictions and other sundry remarks, much to the dismay, embarrassment, and I suspect, secret delight of the people thronging the lobby. The upshot of the incident was that the crew were admonished by their airline with true Scandinavian understanding, and the hotel management saved face by banning that airline's crews from the hotel for six months.

Nothing is or ever will be as good as the "good old days" and I guess that the social lives of airline crews are a perfect example of that. In the old days of the propeller-driven DC-6s, DC-7s, and Constellations, three- or four-day layovers were not uncommon. A crew could find themselves in Madrid for two days, Rome for three, and London for another two. The opportunity for an active social life was great. Sadly, though, with the advent of the Jet Age things began to change. Because of enormous costs, jet airplanes only earn their keep when they are flying passengers and freight around the world. They cannot afford to spend much time on the ground. A crew today consider themselves lucky if they have sufficient time to get to the hotel to shower and eat before going to bed in time to get adequate sleep before leaving on the next leg of the flight. This "quick-turnaround" syndrome has reached the point where pilots are becoming alarmed at the increasing strain and fatigue they are subject to. It is my feeling that pilots have just about reached the fatigue saturation point and any increase in flying time would be highly dangerous.

Finally, a word on that sense of "freedom" many pilots will tell you about, when evaluating their profession. We have two kinds of "freedom." First there is the freedom of a special environment—the sky—and the power and means to play in it. To rise and soar in the air, twist and turn through the majesty of the skies gives us a special understanding of the phrase "free as a bird."

Second, there is that sense of freedom that derives from what is called "command authority." When an airplane is in flight, the captain is by law the master of his vessel, with absolute authority over his airplane, crew, and passengers. He is "free" to make his own decisions, based on his own judgment and experience, on matters of life and death. He commands his own small world. His "freedom" is, paradoxically, his complete responsibility for the plane, its crew and passengers.

You tell me: Is your pilot a man or a superman?

9

Your Stewardess:
More than Meets the Eye

Following World War II, thousands of servicemen returned to their homes after duty in the Far East and Asia. Along with the usual souvenirs—Japanese dolls, kimonos, Samurai swords—they also brought home a dream: ultimate femininity. They had indulged their masculinity in a culture that accepted the obedient servitude of women as the correct order of things. In their most ordinary relationships with Asian women, they were made to feel like princes. Those with a few dollars to spend had become pashas in that shrine of quiet, feminine service, the geisha house.

No sooner had the "Welcome Home" signs and bunting been torn down than they discovered that sweet Mary Lou, the girl they'd left behind, had in their absence become a welder, stevedore, engineer, truck driver, or business-woman. The short supply of men to fill those jobs had successfully accomplished what woman suffrage had failed to do. Worse yet, Mary Lou often actually enjoyed her work and had no intention of handing over her welding torch to her returning hero and quietly slip back into her gingham apron.

The results were nothing short of traumatic. Even as the American GI was winning the fight for democracy a fifth column back home had successfully attacked the bastions of the veterans' masculinity. Because traditional femininity no longer freely abounded, it became a salable commodity. Manufacturers producing all manner of consumer goods pushed their products at the public, using as many pretty bodies and faces as they could get their hands on to help sell their automobiles, lawnmowers, and boats. At the annual automobile show, the bathing beauties outnumbered the cars ten to one.

At the same time this exploitation of femininity was sweeping the country, the demand for commercial transportation increased at an astonishing rate. In the United States alone, nearly 13 million passengers were carried in 1946, an increase of 2,500 percent in twenty years.

Airlines began to compete fiercely with each other in an effort to capture the lion's share of the market for themselves. In the process they came up with the ultimate sales-pitch—the stewardess. High-altitude sex appeal became the most effective weapon in the war for passengers.

The first stewardesses actually took to the air on May 15, 1930—all eight of them. Up until that time, the job of handing out sandwiches, or airsickness bags, fell to the copilot. As airplanes became more complex, they required more attention from the pilots. Airline managements realized that the copilot could be more useful in the cockpit than back in the cabin holding a passenger's hand. Additional crew members to care for the passengers were needed.

Reasonably enough, airline managers wished to provide this service as cheaply as possible. Since slavery had long been abolished and child-labor laws were strictly enforced, what were they to do? What members of society would work like slaves and have the financial requirements of children? The answer was obvious: women.

Women had long been recognized as having the

strength and fortitude for doing menial tasks, and it was thought they only needed enough money to supply themselves with cosmetics, stockings, and other unnecessary things to amuse themselves. Thus, the stewardess made her debut on the aviation scene: conceived from necessity and born of economy.

She was almost called an "airess" or an "airette." Other names suggested were "purserette," "airaide," and "courierette." We can thank God and some unknown airline official that all these were rejected for the name by which we know her today: "stewardess" and, sometimes, "hostess." This designation was chosen over the others because, just like the steward on steamships and railroads, her primary function was to serve the passengers and she has been serving ever since. However, a lot has changed since those early days.

The first airline to employ women as stewardesses was Boeing Air Transport, a predecessor of United Airlines. Boeing required that the women be registered nurses, not only in case of illness among the passengers in flight, but, as one official said, "We want institutionally trained persons accustomed to discipline, since discipline must be paramount at all times." He might also have added that registered nurses made starvation wages at the time.

The other requirements were not much different from those existing today. Applicants could not be over twenty-five years of age, weigh more than 115 pounds, or be taller than five feet four inches. A major airline reports that the average stewardess being hired today is "a bit younger and a mite heavier" than in 1930. In 1930, educational requirements for an airline stewardess did not have to be specified; that she was educationally qualified was implicit in her nurse status.

How surprised those Boeing officials would be if they could see what a stewardess has become today! Surrogate mother, wife, mistress, confessor, and whipping boy (or should that be "whipping girl"?). Their only concern then was to get the maximum amount of flight duty for the minimum amount of pay. Because there was no conception of the stewardess as a sex symbol, she was required to perform a number of "unsexy" duties. Besides catering to the needs of the airline passengers, she helped with the baggage, punched tickets, hauled hampers of food on board, and cleaned up the cabins. Some of the duties would seem very bizarre to today's stewardesses. For example, early stewardesses formed bucket brigades to assist in refueling or helped push planes in and out of hangars. They also wound and set the cabin clock, adjusted the altimeter at each stop, and checked the air speedometers in the main cabin. How different from the squeaky-clean, attractively dressed, smiling stewardesses we expect to find on our flights today! At least, on the surface.

With the increases in aviation, the airplanes became larger, more passengers traveled, more stewardesses were required, and regulations increased.

According to Federal Air Regulation 121–391, a stewardess is on board specifically and primarily "to provide the most efficient egress of passengers in the event of an emergency evacuation." The number of cabin attendants and even their location during takeoff and landing are now governed by federal law. Emergency exits have to be provided in cabins and emergency equipment installed. Today's airplanes, of course, carry an enormous quantity of such equipment. On an overseas flight, for example, you will find concealed in various overhead and behind-the-seat hatches, several huge inflatable rafts containing flares, radio signaling devices, emergency rations, desalting and water-distilling equipment, visual signaling devices, survival manuals, shark repellent, fishing gear, and a multitude of other survival aids. In addition to portable emergency oxygen equipment and first-aid kits, there are several fire extinguishers of different types, each designed to combat different types of fires. The normal and emergency doors are equipped with inflatable escape slides and ropes. In short, every conceivable type of accident situation and its subsequent survival phase has been planned for. Who is responsible for this safety equipment and the carrying out of emergency procedures? Believe it or not, the woman who serves you coffee, tea, or milk.

Serving meals and drinks is only *secondary* to passenger safety. The apparent image of the stewardess may have changed from those rough-and-ready days of early aviation, but that well-groomed, apparently fragile young woman is still highly trained and expected to perform many critical tasks. Next time you are being pampered and cosseted on an airplane, try to imagine your stewardess pulling eighty-pound life rafts from the ceiling, launching and inflating them, taking command of the occupants, and operating the search-and-survival equipment. The odds against her having to do so may be millions to one, but believe me, she could do it and do it well!

There has never been a single case of a stewardess failing to perform her duties in the rare instances when an airplane has had to make a forced landing. In fact, stewardesses have performed above and beyond what is expected of them by going back into a flaming wreckage time and time again to rescue trapped passengers, sometimes at the cost of their own lives.

I have given you a picture of the stewardess as a professional, but what of her other images? The airlines seem to concentrate at least as much of their emphasis and training on the sex-symbol facet as they do on the stewardess' primary function. The marketing and advertising divisions of the airlines appear to rely almost exclusively on the salability of a pretty face. As much agonizing thought, research, and argument goes into the selection of stewardesses' uniforms as into the purchasing of a new fleet of multi-million-dollar airplanes. Despite that, I have yet to find a uniform that was liked by more than 10 percent of the women who had to wear it.

Many changes in the last few years indicate that airline management is stepping up its sex-appeal war. At one time, a woman's hair had to be cut so as not to fall below her shoulders. Girdles were required and eyeglasses banned. Only one shade of lipstick was permitted. On TWA, for instance, the shade was restricted to a lipstick that exactly matched the color in the TWA emblem. No matter what a woman's hair color or complexion, "fire-engine red" lips were required. Under pressure from airline marketing and advertising division and the stewardesses themselves, these ridiculous regulations were relaxed and, judging from the women we see on our airplanes today, with splendid results.

It is to the eternal credit of a handful of dedicated women that even more ridiculous regulations have been lifted. Getting married or becoming pregnant were once both grounds for instant dismissal. Being black didn't get you dismissed because you were never hired in the first place. Most airlines automatically fired their stewardesses when they reached the doddering age of thirty-five. As an official of American Airlines argued in court, "The stewardess position is primarily of interest to young women. The stewardess has become the image of the industry, symbolizing the youth and vitality of the airlines; the stewardess's job requires enthusiasm that is lost with age, and women between the ages of thirty-eight and fifty undergo changes of body, personality, and emotional reactions which would interfere with the performance of the stewardess's job." That was in 1968!

Management's attitude toward their passengers can best be described as "Hefner-esque." They try desperately to create a "flying playboy club" atmosphere. They complete the bunny image by enforcing a "look-but-do-not-touch" rule. Stewardesses have become increasingly dissatisfied with this treatment. An organization called Stewardesses for Women's Rights has been launched. It was founded by two former Eastern stewardesses who quit their jobs after disputes with the management over arbitrary grooming rules. While significant advances have been made with regard to their complaints, they still have a long way to go.

Most of the nation's cabin personnel are organized under two labor unions, the Air Line Steward and Stewardesses Association (ALSSA) and the Steward and Stewardesses Division of the Air Line Pilots Association. The relationship between the two groups might best be described as frosty. To achieve their professional goals it is inevitable that some alliance or merger of the two will take place.

One difficulty both groups face is the short career span of many stewardesses—on average, two years. Most of the women do not concern themselves with what is happening in their organization. Instead, they leave all the work to the 10 percent who do plan long careers in the profession.

Ironically, at the same time as women's rights are being fought for, male liberation has crept up on management officials. A recent court decision obliges airlines to hire cabin attendants without regard to sex. As a result, more and more "welcome-aboard" smiles are likely to shine from a background of five-o'clock shadow!

All kidding aside, I have found this pioneer breed of male cabin attendants to be just as efficient as their female counterparts—though of course I don't find them as attractive. Judging from the amorous adventures of the bachelors among them, I would say that any doubts cast upon their masculinity stem from envy rather than fact. Putting men in a profession predominantly staffed with beautiful women is like rearing foxes in a chicken house. On the other hand, like their female counterparts many enter the profession with the intention of making it a career, and are steady, reliable, married men.

Stewardesses often quit to get married and have children, but sometimes simply because they're disenchanted. Perhaps you are surprised that an attractive single woman could become disenchanted with what on the surface seems like such a desirable job? Here again, there is more than meets the eye.

You *do* meet celebrities, and you *do* travel the world. Certainly the job has glamour. But there is another side to the picture.

You must constantly keep up your appearance. Endless grooming and hairsetting is often conducted with a pocketbook full of makeup and equipment in a small hotel room. There is a perpetual struggle to maintain weight below the arbitrary level set by the airlines. If you get caught in one of the frequent weight-checks and find yourself exceeding the limit, you may find yourself "on the beach" without pay for a couple of weeks, while you desperately struggle to slim down to the point where you fit into the airline height-weight chart.

Having gotten yourself looking perfect, you prepare yourself for a romantic assult on the hundreds of movie and TV actors, rock stars, sports figures, and millionaires who spend half their lives sitting in airplanes. I have met hundreds of celebrities in my career and have found many of them to be charming and intelligent. For those who aren't I can only say that for crude and insulting behavior they have got ordinary passengers beat by a country mile. The stewardess soon discovers that most of the nice ones are married, homosexual, too busy, or just not interested. After the hero of a TV series has bawled her out for the fifth time for screwing up his martini, our celebrity-seeking stewardess is ready to ram it down his throat, glass and all. Disillusion replaces hope, blind hatred replaces hero-worship, and another stewardess bites the dust.

But what about the excitement of travel? Let me describe a typical few days in the life of a stewardess. Lying in a hot bath, face covered with two pounds of cream, ignoring the chatter of the five other "stews" she shares the one-bedroom apartment with, she suddenly gets called to the telephone with those dreaded words, "Bernice, crew schedule wants you." Fifteen minutes later she is scurrying across town to the airline bus terminal, clutching her suitcase and trying to pull up her panty hose. Breathlessly arriving at the airport, she sneaks by the supervisor who checks her for grooming, signs herself in for the flight, and rushes off to the airplane. Seven hours, 400 meals, and three airplane changes later, she collapses on the bed of some hotel in Dayton, Ohio, praying desperately that the nice-looking passenger she made a dinner date with will break his leg on the way to his hotel, or at least get a surprise visit from the wife she suspects he has. Mention the excitement of travel to this gal and you are likely to get your coffee dumped right in your lap.

Of course not *all* days are like this one. But until you have reached some seniority on the job, that is likely to be your unhappy lot. If the stewardess survives this phase of her career, she will then fly a regular schedule of her choice and generally be able to exploit fully the advantages of her job.

The most advantageous part of the job is the free and reduced travel rate. While it may be true that short layovers mean a stewardess has little time for sightseeing or social life, she does only work an average of fifteen days each month. By judicious wheeling and dealing, swapping flights with other women, and using any other means she can think of, she can get her days off in large chunks. If she has enough seniority she probably can get ten days off in a row. This means that each month she has as much time off as most working people get once a year for vacation. Not only does she have the time but also the means to go anyplace in the world. Depending upon her airline she even gets a number of free passes each year. On other airlines, she can obtain reduced fares, 50 to 90 percent off. In addition, she can get greatly reduced hotel rates around the world. Excluding meals and entertainment expenses, a stewardess could fly from New York to Madrid and back, stay in a first-class hotel for a week, and still have spent less than $100. Even in these days of bargain travel packages, that is hard to beat. Most stewardesses do take some advantage of this happy situation and take at least three vacations every year.

When they are not flying or vacationing, some stewardesses run businesses. I am acquainted with several who operate a costume jewelry store, an art store, and a candle store, respectively. Others engage in social or nursing work and other charitable pursuits. The rest do the usual things many single young women do with their free time, such as enjoying their friends, going out on dates, taking a course, or learning a new skill.

Your Stewardess: More than Meets the Eye

Movie houses these days are showing a great many "stewardess movies," where unbridled passion and lust at 40,000 feet are depicted as commonplace. I hate to shatter anyone's private dreams but the truth must be told from personal observation: During many years of flying I haven't met a single woman who could match the performance of her surrogate sisters in those sizzling movie epics.

Of course, a few airline pilots enjoying the locker-room camaraderie of a few drinks with their buddies will tell tales of orgiastic layovers that would gladden the heart and quicken the pulse of any red-blooded voyeur. It has been my experience, however, that these revels always took place "back in the good old days."

Although the "good old days" may no longer be with us, the modern stewardess retains many qualities usually associated with them. No matter how long the flight, how rude the passengers, or how turbulent the weather, at least one of the stewardesses will always lighten the atmosphere with her ready wit. This quickness of tongue also comes in handy when dealing with the unwanted advances of some of her passengers. One woman I know puts them off by giving them a phone number and telling them to call later for a date. The anxious Lothario's hopes soon crash to ground zero when he finds himself listening to Dial-a-Prayer.

I hope that the next time you fly, you will look at your stewardess with different eyes. Remember, if you do have the misfortune to have an accident, she is the one most likely to save your life. Her attractive looks and obliging service are just a bonus. "Would you care for some more coffee, sir?"

10

How Safe Is *Flying?*

For quite some time now, a well-known axiom has been: What goes up, must come down. With the advent of the Space Age that particular saying was removed from our list of maxims. However, to those of us living and working within the gravitational pull of planet Earth, it still remains true.

Every day, throughout the world, this axiom is demonstrated by thousands of airplanes that continue to go up, and come down. The circumstances of their coming down rarely elicit any attention. What newspaper editor would approve a headline reading: JET AIRLINER LANDS SAFELY AFTER ROUTINE FLIGHT?

However, let one airliner come down in a place other than an airport, or in separate pieces, and world wars and other disasters are shoved aside to make room for its appearance on the front page. Why? The death toll from automobile accidents, cancer, heart disease, and accidental shootings is thousands of times greater; what gives an airline crash such newsworthy prominence?

For openers, I suspect that the world has not yet fully accepted flight as a normal occurrence. A small subconscious voice within us says: "There, I told you so. Man shouldn't fool around in the sky. It's not natural."

Another newsworthy feature of a crash is the relatively large number of victims involved.

Perhaps the most telling reason airplane crashes make newspaper headlines is that at the time of an accident, the reasons for the crash are very seldom known. It takes many months of painstaking investigation before the real or probable causes are published. This mystery excites wild speculation on the part of reporters and editors, leading them to point an accusing finger, or make a hero out of a pilot or passenger or stewardess.

On one occasion I was the undeserving recipient of a newspaper reporter's admiration. Some years ago during my military career I crash-landed a jet fighter into a cornfield. The newspaper account the following day went something like this: ". . . after vainly trying to extinguish the fire that was consuming his craft, the young pilot bravely stayed at the controls of the stricken airplane to miss a nursery school and a hospital in the path of its earthward plunge."

What really happened? My engine caught fire because of a broken fuel line. After my attempts to extinguish the fire had failed, I decided that I wanted to rapidly part company with it. I pulled the firing handle on my ejection seat, which should have thrown me clear of the airplane. Unfortunately, the ejection mechanism failed to function correctly. By now I was too low and too chicken to attempt a manual departure "over the side," so with no other choice left, I stayed with the airplane and crash-landed it into a field without too much damage to myself. I do recall avoiding a couple of buildings, neither of which I recognized as a school or hospital, so I wouldn't come to a sudden stop into the side of one of them. Besides that, the newspaper spelled my name wrong.

Before the Jet Age, almost all airline crashes were written off as "probable cause—pilot error" unless overwhelming evidence to the contrary was available. When the first jets appeared, "crashproof black boxes" were installed, which record flight information such as speed, altitude, attitude, rates of climb or descent, and so forth. In addition, a cockpit voice recorder tapes all conversation that takes place in the cockpit. (Actually the "black boxes" are painted a bright orange or yellow to assist in their location at crash sites.) Using this recorded data, an experienced crash investigation team can reconstruct every minute of an airplane's flight. The most modern jets include instruments that record changes in engine speed, and keep track of who was at the controls at any given time.

As a result, the number of "probable-cause—pilot-error" verdicts have dropped sharply. I am not suggesting that pilots never make errors, but it is extremely rare that they make a *fatal* one. Remember, they want to stay alive, too. I am justifiably proud of my colleagues who on many occasions have brought crippled airplanes to a safe landing. I say this not only as a pilot but also as a certified accident investigator.

The major cause of accidents today is mechanical malfunction. Airplanes are designed and maintained with great care and include a number of back-up systems, but unfortunately mechanical failures sometimes do occur. While realizing that perfection is impossible, airplane manufacturers and airlines still aim for it. With the aid of new methods and tools for anticipating mechanical failures long before they actually occur, we are daily closing the gap between the "impossible" and reality.

One chink in the armor of airline safety is the absence of Instrument Landing Systems (ILS) and crash and rescue facilities at some airports. Although most major airports are adequately equipped, airports of small or medium-size cities may not be. ILS should be installed at all commercial airports. Most pilots faced with a potential crash landing will invariably choose a military airport where they know that the best crash and rescue facilities are available.

There is one last possible cause of airplane accidents: "an act of God." This is a catch-all phrase used to describe sudden freak weather conditions that range from bird strikes to being hit by meteorites. (I must confess that I have never heard of an accident occurring as a result of the latter.) A couple of books in the last twenty years have advanced the theory that the disappearance of several (mostly military) airplanes can be explained by their having been hijacked by vessels from outer space. I have to admit that in the face of this extraterrestrial threat, the airlines are powerless!

In trying to describe what can cause airplane accidents I have, no doubt, thoroughly alarmed you. To get things back into perspective, let's take a look at some of the facts. *How often* do accidents occur?

In the United States alone, more than half a million passengers, from 524 airports, board 2,500 airplanes for an average journey of 600 miles, EVERY DAY. Multiply that by 365 and you will arrive at a substantial number of people flying a great number of miles on a large number of airplanes each year. How many air disasters do you read about each year? Two? Three? Maybe even four. Airplane safety statistics are compiled on the basis of "passenger-seat miles." That is, the number of miles flown by the airline multiplied by the seats they had available on those flights. In 1972, for every 100 million passenger-seat miles traveled on all domestic and international flights by U.S. carriers, 0.13 accidental deaths occurred.

If only a small portion of the apprehension and cautious respect for flying could be transferred to automobiles, maybe some of the bloodshed on our roads would be reduced. Does it frighten you to drive to the supermarket? Well, it should; you stand a greater chance of death or injury on that short ride than I face in an entire lifetime in the cockpit of an airplane.

Hopefully, I have convinced you that you will not be involved in an accident when you fly. Now I will explode your confidence by giving you some advice on surviving one should it occur!

It is a fact that the overwhelming majority of airplane accidents are survivable. If the pilot has any sort of control left by the time the airplane arrives on the surface, the fuselage will usually remain intact or, at worst, break in two at the final stages of the landing run. If you know what to do, you will walk away from the wreck.

When you first board an airplane, take particular note of the exit nearest your seat. (See Chapter 1.) If after a crash landing you can see fire outside your nearest exit, *do not* open that door. The fire is likely to spill into the cabin. Find a door that opens onto a safe area.

Above all, DON'T PANIC. Your cockpit and cabin crew are superbly trained to handle emergency situations, so follow their instructions. Move quickly but deliberately. Do not attempt to take anything with you on an emergency evacuation. I know of a case recently where a passenger evacuated down an emergency slide carrying his two bottles of duty-free liquor. Of course, when he hit the ground both bottles broke and passengers and crew members who followed him down the slide were severely cut by the broken glass.

Most passengers react with understandable concern

when the captain announces that the plane is turning back due to a "minor mechanical malfunction." They immediately assume that he is lying to them and in fact the airplane is about to fall apart.

Most airline pilots know that lying to the passengers can work against them. If a pilot has serious problems, he wants his passengers prepared so that an orderly, successful evacuation can take place when the airplane lands. If he says it's minor—believe him.

He is perfectly capable of flying a two- or three-engine airplane on one engine; a four-engine airplane will fly comfortably on two. He can fly and land his airplane without electrical power, hydraulic power, even without landing gear, and what's more, he can do it in such a way that you can all discuss it over a martini later.

Large financial concerns, such as insurance companies, are noted for their practical, conservative approach to their investments. It is very significant that the rates for life and accident insurance are no higher for an airline pilot than for an accountant or gardener.

So relax. If I get there—so will you.

11

Planesmanship

It is an irony that air travel, which is glamorous and romantic, should begin in airports, which are not. Airports are the limbo of the travel world where travelers are forced to wait in the maw of some awesome machine, having not yet departed, nor yet arrived.

The constant ebb and flow of traveling humanity washing through the halls and lounges creates the nearest thing to perpetual motion. Airports never sleep. An airport is a place of strangeness and strangers. People's inhibitions fall from them like scales. Love, hate, greed, fear abound in the departure lounge. Some people become children, to be led gently by the hand. Others become raving lunatics. Many, in self-defense, become zombies, completely impervious to the blandishments of the garbled public address system. I have seen travelers just sit with blissfully vacant looks while they were being paged repeatedly.

Once at Fiumicino in Rome I sat in the coffee shop next to a man with a Lisbon boarding pass in his pocket. His flight was called, and he continued sipping his coffee. The flight was called again, more urgently. He didn't move. After a final, desperate call, I tapped him on the arm and said, "Excuse me, but aren't you going to Lisbon?" He looked at me blankly and replied, "No, actually I am going to Portugal."

In an airport all the suppressed anger of an insecure world comes close to the surface. I have seen mild-mannered and inoffensive people explode in an outburst of fury at the most trifling delay. It is the environment that produces this Jekyll-and-Hyde characteristic, an environment populated by transients, and rendered impermanent by the constant alterations and rebuilding that seem to exist at every airport in the world. Adding to the confusion is the "nonspeak" which pours from the loudspeakers of the public address system. The announcers have developed a lingua franca of their own. Over the years they have memorized announcements in three or four languages, none of which they speak, and with the passage of time these announcements have blended together in a kind of aviation Esperanto which only they can understand.

Airports, which should be painless stopovers between cities, are instead psychic obstacle courses. I hope to provide you with enough information to survive their assault on your sanity and emerge with your nerves, sense of humor, and most of your money intact.

The commodity the airlines deal with is people, who come in all sizes, weights, temperaments, appetites, habits, charms, and quirks. Few of these people have the vaguest idea of what to do in relation to air travel, so the airlines take over as "Big Brother," and tell them what to pay, where to sit, what to do—and ask that they do it without complaining.

Unless you can afford your own airplane there is no way you can avoid being thrust into this system; but once in it, a smart traveler finds ways of exploiting it.

Planesmanship is a kind of traveling game that you play to your own advantage. It begins long before you ever step into an airport terminal.

When you are planning a trip one of the major considerations is the price of the ticket. Contrary to popular
belief, all airlines do not charge the same amount for any
given flight on any day. There are literally dozens of bargains that can save you anywhere from a few dollars up to
half the full published fare.

The variety and complexity of the airline fare structure
would make an IBM 360 computer blow a diode. For example, for a flight between Washington, D.C., and Honolulu there are exactly fifty different fares published! The
differences in price range from a couple of dollars all the
way up to eighty-six dollars. If you go to a ticket counter in
Washington, D.C., and purchase a ticket to Honolulu, it's a
good bet that you will be charged the premium fare, unless
you know better.

The fault does not necessarily lie with the agent selling
you your ticket. In recent years his airline and all the others
have "gone forth and multiplied" in the field of special
airfares. Just to give you an idea, there are special fares for
children traveling alone, children accompanied by an
adult, senior citizens, clergy, families, students, and the
military. There are standby fares for the military, youths,
and adults. Lower prices abound in tour fares, Visit U.S.A.
fares, Discover America fares, night fares, stopover fares
(where you may break your journey at an intermediate city
not geographically located in a straight line between your
point of departure and final destination), and joint fares to
be utilized by you and your husband or wife.

The last one can be the most dangerous. I know of
several instances where businessmen have taken their sec-
retaries or "assistants" on trips with them and have utilized
the joint fare. When their wives received a promotional
letter from the airline asking them how they enjoyed the
trip, the dollars saved were soon swallowed up in the cost

of the divorce or the purchase of a placating mink coat!

If you are traveling on business or on a rigid time schedule, it is unlikely that you will be able to take advantage of any special fare. If, however, your plans are more flexible and you are traveling with your family, it is a good bet that by a little judicious juggling of your departure and return dates you can qualify for one of the excursion fares most airlines offer. Excursion fares or economy round-trip tickets offer reductions if you stay away for a certain minimum and maximum number of days, say fourteen to twenty-one days. Further reductions may be available for longer periods of twenty-two to forty-five days. In addition, if you depart and return on certain weekdays, further reductions may be made.

If you have some flexibility in your travel plans, shop around carefully among the airlines or travel agents. Tell them you are not tied to a rigid schedule and tell them you wish to take advantage of any special fares you might qualify for by a slight readjustment of your travel days.

Such arrangements mean extra time for the reservations agent because he must research his fare structure, so it is advisable that you call during his slack times. These generally exist between midnight and 7:00 A.M. and between 5:30 and 6:30 P.M. You can also, at your leisure, get a travel agent in your local town to do the research and ticketing for you.

If you intend to do it this way, I would point out a couple of things. All of these special fares apply only to tourist- or coach-class travel; first-class fares remain the same whatever day or time you fly or whoever you are. Second, don't let a supercilious ticket agent con you into thinking that you may get third-rate service, an unguaranteed seat, or any other unsatisfactory treatment because you requested a "discount fare." There is no such thing as a

118

"discount fare." If you meet the requirements for, let's say, a military nighttime standby ticket, the price of that ticket is the absolute *maximum* you may be charged. Any higher fare is an illegal overcharge and according to the Civil Aeronautics Board, which regulates the airlines, such an illegal charge will cost the offending airline a thousand-dollar fine.

In addition to the standing or permanent special fares, airlines are permitted to introduce "promotional fares." These usually incorporate a package deal of hotel room, car rental, etc. They certainly seem very attractive, but traveler beware; some of them are impossible to accomplish. A recent offering for a five-day round trip to Jamaica and Nassau could only be used on Tuesdays, coming and going. Only by rewriting the calendar could anyone arrange a five-day trip starting and ending on those days. Examples of similar idiocies are numerous though I suspect they are usually the result of gross stupidity, or carelessness, rather than deliberate fraud.

In many instances the ticket agent is not to blame for overcharging. To arrive at the correct fare it is necessary for him to interview the passenger before issuing the ticket. This is one area where you can help him and possibly save yourself some money. Avoid purchasing your ticket at busy airline counters, particularly at airports. Use the services of a travel agent or purchase your ticket in advance at the future-date counter. Get a quote on your fare from at least two airlines. Tell them *all* the pertinent details about yourself and those traveling with you. Make a note of the name of the agent quoting the fare.

If your itinerary permits, try to stay with one airline and purchase all your tickets at the same time. This way you may qualify for further reductions in price. If your plans are tentative regarding return or onward flight dates, purchase open-ended tickets. Finally, if you are traveling between two points, both within California, do not purchase tickets for that trip outside of that state. While airline tariffs are regulated by the CAB, a unique California state law permits price competition between points within the state. Buying a Los Angeles–San Francisco ticket in Denver would cost you $22. The same ticket purchased in Los Angeles is $16.50, almost a 25 percent saving.° So, next time you plan to fly, if you have sufficient notice, take the time to ensure that you are getting the most for your money by following these suggestions. The airlines won't cheat you deliberately; just don't give them the chance to do it inadvertently.

Just how do you select an airline? If you are a regular traveler, you no doubt already have a favorite airline and will stick with it as long as it behaves itself. Apart from personal choice or whim, there are several factors to consider when deciding whom to give your business to. The choice is not easy since almost all airlines are members of national and international associations and are bound by rigid agreements about what they can offer passengers.

These agreements specify, for example, that noncharter fares are the same on any given airline for any given flight. The quantity of food and other goodies dispensed en route and how often they are to be served are fixed by agreement, so that doesn't help you either. Each airline will advertise the yummiest meals, stewardesses with the brightest smiles, and captains with the steeliest eyes. Conditioned by years of TV commercials, you don't believe that either. The safety record of all U.S. air carriers is outstanding and about the same for each one, so you get no help there.

° At the time of writing—may be subject to change.

120

If you have no past experience to go on, you will probably canvass your friends for recommendations. There are a bewilderingly large number of airlines serving the same places but some have acquired a reputation for dealing best with a certain segment of the traveling public. American Airlines, for instance, has a reputation for handling businessmen, TWA for their attention to families, Pan American for first-class passengers. I have sampled all of these airlines in all of these passenger roles, and frankly cannot find sufficient consistency to confirm their reputations.

One important point to consider when deciding on an airline is whether it permits carry-on baggage to be stowed in special cabin compartments. If you are in a hurry or have a short time between connecting flights, you can walk right off the airplane with your baggage and avoid any baggage-handling delays. All airlines permit you to stow a carry-on bag beneath your seat. This is most convenient if you are able to pack your clothing needs into a bag that measures approximately 13 by 9 inches. On a businessman's flight between New York and Chicago, I doubt that more than 10 percent of the passengers have baggage in the cargo hold of the airplane.

It is also convenient to keep your baggage with you in case you encounter a mechanical delay prior to departure. You may be able to transfer yourself to another airline but getting your suitcase out of the cargo hold of the delayed airplane is virtually impossible under these circumstances.

The main disadvantage of staying with your baggage, apart from sometimes having to carry it long distances, is that it will have to be examined in the security checks that are now conducted at all U.S. airports and many overseas terminals. But this is a small price to pay for the convenience.

For international flights one final consideration in choosing your airline is whether it has its own international arrival terminal in the United States complete with its own body of customs and immigration offiicials. The bedlam surrounding the simultaneous arrival of ten airplanes from ten different countries at the same terminal building can give anyone a headache and certainly adds time to getting home.

If you do not have a favorite airline, this question may help you in making a choice: Which airline operates non-stop to your destination? Intermediate stops can add a considerable amount of time to your trip, and you stand a greater chance of being grounded due to mechanical delays. There are many component parts and systems on an airplane that may malfunction in flight without creating a serious problem. They may be, however, of such a nature that they must be corrected at the next point of landing. If you are on a nonstop flight, that means you will not be exposed to a mechanical delay. If you have an intermediate stop to make, a delay at best could mean an hour or two, and at worst, cancellation of the onward portion of your flight.

Whenever making travel arrangements with a rigid time schedule, always attempt to book flights that originate at your point of departure. For example, if you are traveling from Chicago to Los Angeles, select a flight that originates in Chicago. If it is coming through, say, from New York, it is entirely possible that it could be delayed due to bad weather on the East Coast. It is most frustrating to sit around on a beautiful, sunny day waiting several hours for a flight that has been delayed due to bad weather. A smart traveler also allows himself an absolute minimum of one and a half hours for an intermediate connection.

If you have to get to your destination today, avoid booking on the last flight out. If bad weather or a mechanical malfunction delay an earlier flight you can always switch to a later one—unless the flight you booked is the last one out that day.

Whatever flight you select, when you check in for your originating flight, check your baggage through to your final destination. If your second flight is on a different airline, just request that your baggage be transported swiftly to your next flight. Otherwise you may end up dragging your pile of baggage from one airline check-in counter to another.

One thing to be aware of before booking your flight is the split-terminal situation that often exists in large cities. For example, you may take one airline from Dayton, Ohio, to New York, and expect to depart on another airline from New York to Paris. Having allowed one and a half hours for your connection, you find to your horror that the Dayton–New York flight lands in New York all right, but at La Guardia Airport. Your Paris flight departs from John F. Kennedy International Airport. They both serve New York City, but are seven miles apart. Seven miles in New York during rush hour can take more than an hour to travel.

Other major airports in the United States with split terminals include Chicago (O'Hare-Midway) and San Francisco (San Francisco International–Oakland). Abroad, there are Rome (Fiumicino-Champino), Milan (Malpensa-Linate), London (Heathrow-Gatwick), and Paris (Orly-Le Bourget).

In planning your journey you should take into consideration what local time you will arrive at your destination. Because of different time zones around the world, you could find yourself fighting your way to your departure airport during the evening rush hour and arriving at your destination in time to fight your way to your hotel through the morning rush hour. The next forty-eight hours will probably be spent lying on your hotel bed in a state of nervous exhaustion. The repeated traffic jam, combined with a long air journey, should be enough to achieve this, but if it fails to dampen your spirits, the effects of dysrhythmia, or jet lag, certainly will.

What is jet lag? It is a name for what happens to a person when his biological functions, attuned by daily habit to his home environment, are transported suddenly to a longitudinal outskirt of the world. There, his system is disrupted because he is out of concert with his new locale psychologically and physiologically.

Does it really have any important effects? Well, there was speculation that dysrhythmia reduced Nikita Khrushchev to shoe-banging rudeness at the United Nations several years ago. Who can predict, for instance, the consequence on a future Henry Kissinger who is out of sorts at a conference of international importance?

I do know that jet lag can seriously cripple the beginning of a tightly planned vacation or vital business trip.

Perhaps the effects of jet lag can be minimized by understanding what actually happens to the human body when traveling from west to east or vice versa.

In all of us, an internal biological clock controls our pulse rate, body temperature, and a variety of subtle, biochemical inputs and reactions, according to our regular waking and sleeping hours.

At night our pulse slows, our temperature drops, and hormones and enzymes ebb. We slip into low gear, resting for the demands of the next day.

In the morning, when we wake up, a tide of chemicals surges into the brain, the muscles, and all the systems that activate our basic bodily functions. Our liver is signaled by enzymes to begin the work of eliminating waste from the blood. The stomach's digestive fluids prepare for breakfast. Our urinary and renal functions react to habit and daily demands. Day after day, night after night, the basic twenty-four-hour cycle of our life-style repeats itself and, in effect, winds up our body clock.

Suddenly we are jetborne to Europe or Asia, and an abrupt shift occurs in the time zone and our pattern of living. Our body clock is bewildered. By habit, it strives to maintain its hometown habits. We are awake in London, when we should be asleep in Chicago. We're dining in Hong Kong when our stomach should be empty and resting in Los Angeles. Our pulse rate struggles to maintain the old hometown beat for sleeping in the face of the faster daytime rhythm of activity. Odd reactions set in. Our handshake is weaker. We find it diffiicult to remember familiar names, known dates, where we put our passport, the hotel key, and even what day and time it is.

A great deal of research has been conducted into the cause and effects of this malaise. The medical department of TWA performed controlled experiments with fourteen travelers as guinea pigs. From these experiments, they were able to arrive at certain conclusions and make specific recommendations for methods of overcoming the effects of jet lag.

Based on these findings, and my own experience, I recommend that you take the following steps to minimize its effects:

Avoid full meals or more than a normal amount of alcoholic consumption not only on your flight but after you reach your destination.

If your body clock is attuned to sleep, curl up in the airplane, if you are able, and snooze for a while. You will be in better shape when you arrive to face a daytime existence, even when your body is on sleep time at home. Or if you should be awake, stay awake and sleep when you arrive.

Try to stay on your own time the first day or so in a strange place, sneaking a little extra sleep to prepare your body for a transition to its new time environment.

Avoid the use of medicines at times other than those that your body clock is used to handling. Diabetics and others on repeated medications should alert their physicians to their travel plans and obtain advice on medication.

Above all, ease into your new environment. Avoid too abrupt a change. If you are in London after a trip from New York, for example, for the first day don't do business at 9:00 A.M. London time. Instead, delay your important appointments til 3:00 or 4:00 in the afternoon when you are at peak efficiency, both mentally and physically. That night go to bed a couple of hours later. Gradually work into London's time and help your body clock reset itself to the new demands.

If time does not permit you to take advantage of these suggestions, try to prepare yourself prior to your departure by adjusting yourself to a schedule closer to the time of your destination.

Airline pilots who spend a large part of their lives rushing back and forth between time zones suffer the same debilitating effects as the inexperienced traveler. They, however, do not find strange places so new and exciting, which is part of the dysrhythmia syndrome. While on duty,

I have occasionally flown completely around the world within a ten-day period. As my family and friends can testify, I still become time-disoriented for at least two days following my return. Less experienced travelers may often be affected by jet lag for up to a week, or more!

If you are on vacation and have a flight of more than six hours, the best way to get off to a good start is to arrive at your destination about midmorning. Get to your hotel, unpack, and *go to bed*. Sleep for four or five hours (you will find this easy, believe me) and then force yourself to get up (this you will find difficult).

You will feel terrible for about an hour after you get up but by the time you start feeling human again you are ready for an evening cocktail, dinner, and a leisurely appraisal of your new surroundings. By the time you go to bed again that night, you will have slipped (almost) painlessly into the local time routine. After many years of experiment I have found this to be the quickest possible method of settling in and I know the majority of my fellow pilots would agree.

You have now selected your airline, booked your flight, and are excitedly preparing for your odyssey. I'll make only one suggestion for the selection of clothes you intend to take with you. Take what you need. Don't rely on buying the bulk of your vacation clothing at your destination overseas. There is more than a good chance that you will find the selection too expensive, not to your taste, or of lower quality than obtainable domestically. We all know at least one fellow who found that the "twenty-four-hour" Hong Kong suit he had bought did in fact fall apart at the seams twenty-four hours after he arrived home.

By all means plan to take advantage of special bargains in various countries, such as woolens in England, shoes in

Italy, and leather goods in Spain, but don't plan your entire wardrobe around them.

On the other hand, don't take too many clothes with you. Apart from the inconvenience of lugging half a ton of luggage around, it can cost you a great deal in excess baggage charges. On international flights your free allowance is sixty-six pounds in first class and forty-four pounds in economy. You can fudge it a little, if you carry your heavy coat separately, and some airlines will permit you to get away with a carry-on suit bag in addition to your allowance.

The one airline I know that is very strict on weight limitation is Lufthansa. One woman I know was obliged to have her handbag weighed in with her luggage and counted as part of her allowance. Excess baggage charges are generally quite steep and are calculated as a percentage of the fare, so depending upon the length of your flight you could finish up paying freight on that extra coat in excess of its value.

Customs can cause a lot of headaches among travelers so make sure you don't get charged for anything you may have taken with you from home. You doubtless will take such items as watches, cameras, jewelry, and other valuables. You possibly will also tote along a transistor radio or tape recorder. If the items are new or look new, it is advisable to take receipts with you, to make sure some eagle-eyed customs inspector doesn't charge you duty on them when you return home.

If you cannot find the receipts, you may take the items into customs *before* departure and have them listed and receipted by the customs department. This may save you some time, embarrassment, and possibly money when you return home. Your airline agent can tell you how to find the customs department at your departure airport.

A few last words of advice on packing: If you plan to take a portable radio with you either in your luggage or on your person, disconnect the battery just in case it accidentally switches on. It could affect the navigation instruments on your airplane.

If you are taking aerosol cans with you (shaving cream, for example), seal them firmly in large plastic bags. The not so gentle handling your bags may receive combined with several hours in an unpressurized baggage compartment, could leave you with a suitcase full of soapy foam.

Pack a small carry-on bag to hold your reading material, camera, sunglasses, passports, and other valuables. If you are traveling economy class, take along a pair of stretch slipper socks (they are provided in first class). Your feet will start to swell an hour or so after takeoff and if you don't take off your shoes your journey will be very uncomfortable. Plan to wear loose, comfortable, mediumweight clothing for the trip.

The constantly changing air-conditioned air in the cabin can affect the moisture of your skin. After a short time aloft your skin may dry out and flake in small pieces like dandruff. It is harmless but unsightly, so you may wish to pack a good skin lotion with you and apply it to your exposed skin during the first hour of your flight.

If you are taking medication, be sure that you have an adequate supply for the time you will be away. You may find that you cannot obtain certain drugs in certain countries. In addition, take along a small medical kit with aspirin, antacids, a couple of Band-aids, and paregoric for diarrhea.

Those traveling with pets must give the airline advance notice. There are a number of regulations concerning pets in the cabin. Generally, only one animal may be carried in each section of the cabin, that is, one in first class and one in the coach section. The pets must be transported in a suitable container; if you do not have one, the airline will provide one for a small fee.

Pets may be carried in comfort and safety in one of the cargo holds. At least one cargo hold on each airplane is pressurized and heated for this purpose. This is often the easiest way of transporting your dog or cat, or if you lean to the esoteric, your boa constrictor.

Advice on preparing your pet for its journey will be furnished by the airline. In general, if you stop feeding it twelve hours prior to flight, and give it very little water, it will probably have a dry, odorless journey. It is also advisable to give your pet a tranquilizer that has been prescribed by a veterinarian prior to boarding.

Seeing-eye dogs are not classified as pets. They may travel free of charge with their owners in the cabin.

Reservations made, tickets in hand, sensibly packed, and comfortably dressed, you are ready for your departure from home. How you get from your home to the airport depends upon your personal preference or the availability of public transportation or taxicabs.

If you have convenient taxi or limousine service to the airport, I recommend that you use it because it eliminates parking problems. Remember to allow time for especially heavy traffic.

But many travelers insist on driving to the airport. If you are one of those who do, drive straight to the departure terminal, and leave your wife or husband, children, and baggage at curbside in the charge of a skycap porter.

Next, head for the long-term parking lot, which, with a traveler's luck, is probably a couple of miles away, but *will* save you seven or eight dollars a day.

When you park, write down your car's exact location and put the note in your wallet. After spending two weeks gazing at the Tower of London or the Folies Bergère, you could easily draw a blank when you try to pick out your trusty vehicle from among 6,000 others. You would also be well advised to carry a set of battery-starter cables in the trunk, and depending on the season and your geographic location, a snow shovel. Remember, two or three weeks is a long time to leave your car standing in the open.

All you have left to do is ride the free bus back to the terminal, where, hopefully, you find your baggage has been checked in, and you have time for a cup of coffee or a cocktail before boarding your flight.

A word of warning about "duty-free" shopping. Among the few permanent residents at airports are the worst and rudest traders in the world. Piled high with mountains of useless bric-a-brac and so-called "duty-free" bargains, they lie in wait for the unwary traveler to sell him things he does not need at prices he cannot afford. In many airports, particularly Rome, Beirut, Hong Kong, and Frankfurt, I have seen goods in the so-called duty-free shops that were actually more expensive than their equivalent in the city. In Frankfurt, I was once quoted a duty-free price of $268 on a slide projector I had just purchased downtown for $180.

Some airports, thankfully, do provide reasonable duty-free shops; in particular I recommend Amsterdam's Schipol airport and Shannon in Ireland. In most of the others, I would limit my purchases to duty-free liquor and tobacco, unless you have had a chance to compare the downtown prices.

Arriving at the airport early saves much wear and tear on your nerves. It will also give you a better choice of seats on the airplane. Your seat assignment will in most cases be allocated by the ticket agent at the departure gate. What are the best seats? There are many variables involved in the selection of seats.

You may wish to select them on the basis of smoking or no-smoking sections. If you wish to see the movie, sit at least seven rows back from the screen. Incidentally, there will be a charge to see the movie, usually $2.50. Your money buys you a headset which plugs into a number of sound channels, one of which is for the movie. The others play anything from children's stories to acid rock. I should warn you that the sound reproduction is not very good, and the sets are uncomfortable as well. Why the charge? To pacify those airlines who are unable or unwilling to offer this service.

If you wish to sleep, stay away from the extreme back or front of the cabin where galleys and washrooms are located. A small crowd usually gathers in these areas during flight, either waiting to get into the washroom, or trying to get a date with the stewardesses.

For a good view, get a window seat but avoid those rows adjacent to the wings as you will not be able to see down. If you are traveling economy class, avoid the middle seat in any row, unless you are sharing the row with someone near and dear to you. Being the filling in a human sandwich is rarely pleasant. I usually try to sit as far forward in the cabin as I can because tail seats bear the brunt of any vibration and roughness that may occur in flight. The advice to sit forward is especially pertinent on airplanes that have tail-mounted engines. The harmonic frequency such engines produce could give you quite a headache.

A word on your rights as a ticket holder: It is important that you be aware of the responsibilities the airlines have toward you. When they sell you a ticket and accept your reservation, they commit themselves to getting you to your destination.

Occasionally, difficulties arise in fulfilling that commitment. Although a reasonable person will not hold them responsible for delays or cancellations due to weather, the traveler should know that the airlines are obliged to take care of him during such delays. If your delay or cancellation is caused by something affecting only that particular airline, it must get you on your way to your destination within a specific period of time or pay you monetary compensation. You have the right to request information regarding these time limits from your airline.

If you are traveling first class, it may be useful to remember certain special rights and privileges your ticket allows. There are often times when an airline will overbook the coach or tourist section on a flight. If all the booked passengers do turn up, the airline may move them up, at no additional charge to those extra passengers, to first class. In this event the airline is obliged to refund the first-class surcharge paid by the first-class passengers.

An airline may not necessarily make you aware of this. If you have reason to suspect such a thing has happened (usually one of the lucky "upgrades" will confide his good fortune to you), I suggest you speak to the senior cabin attendant about your entitled refund.

Airline overbooking may also result in latecomers' being turned away despite their confirmed reservations (another good reason to get to the airport early). Plagued by people who book different flights on different airlines on the same day to ensure that they will arrive in time for at least one of them, the airlines automatically allow for a certain number of "no-shows" on every flight. Occasionally their predictions do not work out and they find themselves with a number of irate "oversales" breathing down their necks at the check-in counters.

Most airline employees will admit their responsibility toward you, but on occasion they may try to brush you off. Under those circumstances stand firm and demand that they get you to your destination either on a later flight or on another airline. If you are seriously delayed, you have the right to expect them to provide you with a meal at the airport restaurant. If you are firmly polite, they will soon recognize that you know your rights and cannot be put off by a "that's-your-tough-luck" attitude.

An airline is also responsible for its ticket holder's luggage. If yours is lost or damaged, report it to your airline immediately. If you are overseas and need cash to replace a few essentials while they are trying to find your bag, tell them. They must compensate you for any inconvenience.

Under any of these circumstances, stand firm and tell them to solve your problem. If it is their fault, they must take care of you; your ticket is a contract that they must honor. If the alternate arrangements they make are not to your satisfaction, don't accept them. Most major airlines honor their responsibilities but occasionally you will come up against an overzealous employee whose self-appointed task is to protect his employer from grumbling passengers.

Remember, when you fly—first class, economy, or charter—you are a VIP, protected by laws and regulations, both domestic and international. If you give the airlines a chance, they will usually fall over themselves in an honest attempt to solve your problem. I offer these suggestions, not because you are not smart enough to figure it out for yourself, but because many passengers become understandably bewildered when they walk into an overcrowded, bustling airport terminal.

Once on board you might keep several other things in mind. Consideration of your fellow passengers is the hallmark of an experienced air traveler. If you smoke a pipe or cigar, take a stroll to the gallery area to indulge your habit. Very few people enjoy your pipe or cigar at close range in close quarters.

If you are in a window or middle seat, try to make a trip to the bathroom prior to the time drinks or meals are served. Climbing over two people who are trapped in their seats by trays laden with glasses or meals can be embarrassing to you and a severe annoyance to them.

If religious or dietary considerations make it necessary for you to have special food, give the airline enough notice (about twenty-four hours) and they will provide it for you. It is wise to reiterate your request when you check in for your flight just in case someone has slipped up and failed to order your special meal.

Check behind you before you fully recline your seat, and then do so only if the seat behind you is unoccupied. Remember, the back of your seat occupies a large piece of the space the passenger behind you has; it also provides a meal tray for him. Jerking your seat back and forth makes life uncomfortable for him and is also extremely bad manners. If the seat behind you is occupied and you are traveling in coach, do not recline your seat farther than one notch from the upright position. The seat is very comfortable in that position and the person behind you will certainly appreciate your good traveling manners.

Keep your seat belt loosely fastened when you are seated in case you run into some unexpected turbulence. On several occasions passengers have been slightly hurt because of very light turbulence causing the airplane to suddenly drop a few feet. It also allows you to continue sleeping undisturbed when the seat-belt sign comes on. Otherwise, the stewardess will have to wake you up to ask you to fasten your seat belt.

If you have no other pressing use for it, use the airsickness bag provided in the seat pocket as a trash basket for your litter, facial tissues, candy wrappers, etc. Consideration of these matters will play a large part in making your flight pleasant..

Humorist Robert Benchley observed many years ago that there are only two kinds of travel—first class or with children. With a little planning you can prove him wrong. If you are taking the children along, try to select a flight on one of the jumbo jets where there is more space for them to expend a little energy. The long row of seats makes it possible to have them sit with you and permits a greater degree of parental supervision.

If you cannot travel on a jumbo jet, try to get the row of seats facing the bulkhead in front, which is also close to the galley. There will be no expensive hairstyles or angora sweaters for their sticky fingers to grab when they get up four times an hour to go to the bathroom. Also give them travel-sickness pills before boarding the airplane and in flight avoid feeding them large amounts of candy.

Ask the stewardess to serve their meals first. (An experienced stewardess will do this without being asked.) You will have enough time to open all their wrappings, cut up their food if necessary, and have your own meal in comfort a little later.

I have discovered one thing when traveling with my family that I am at a complete loss to explain. There seems to be a mysteriously direct connection between the FASTEN SEAT BELT sign, and the pressure level in their little bladders. As soon as the sign goes on they immediately have to go to the bathroom. To try to outwit them you might follow this plan. By threats of cajoling, *make* them go to the bathroom (1) as soon as you get on board; (2) just prior to the meal service; and (3) at the commencement of the descent.

If you are traveling with a very small baby, again try to get the forward bulkhead seats and order a sky cot in advance. The airline will provide one free of charge if it has enough notice. Take along dry formula and mix it on board the airplane. Most airlines will not permit their cabin attendants to mix the formula but they will make the galleys available for you to do so. They will prepare strained baby foods for you but it is advisable that you bring your own. One other useful tip—the airsickness bags make perfect containers for soggy diapers.

I have noticed that more and more photography buffs seem to be on board my airplanes. If you wish to indulge in this fascinating hobby while you are flying, I would make some suggestions.

Obviously, you should try to get a window seat. If there is any difficulty or you arrive too late to reserve one, most ticket agents will oblige you if you explain why you want that seat. Try to sit ahead of the engines; directly behind them flows a stream of hot gases that will distort your view.

As for your camera, most professional photographers suggest a single-lens reflex camera with a built-in exposure meter. Since you are shooting into glass it's easy to pick up a reflection. A single-lens reflex shows you when the reflection is visible; with a rangefinder this reflection is more difficult to see. Use black cameras with black lenses. Put black electrical tape over the chrome parts of your camera. The reflection from the sun can be very annoying.

Normal exposure times are thrown off due to the filtered glass. Light reflected from clouds is comparable to that of a bright beach or snowy mountains. A camera with a built-in light meter will make allowances for this. Use wide-angle lenses, 15 to 35 mm. Don't use lenses over 85 to 105 mm; they are just about impossible.

If you use polarized filters, you're likely to get a collection of weird colors from the glass. Use a sky light or ultraviolet filter. They serve a dual purpose—to clear the blue out of the shadows and protect the lens from the sticky fingers of tiny passengers.

The best time to shoot is early morning or late afternoon. During those times, long shadows appear on the ground and the light makes interesting patterns on the ground.

The most fascinating view I have seen from an airplane is an approach to a night landing over a large lit-up city. Alas, you will have to store that picture in your memory. There is not enough light to give a fast exposure.

Cockpit crew members are usually friendly, gregarious people, and they would like to see you, but strict regulations forbid passenger visits to the cockpit during flight. You may, however, arrange a visit to the cockpit prior to your departure or after your arrival. All you need do is ask your stewardess. I would suggest that you make your call before departure as it is usually more convenient and also (hopefully) encouraging for you to meet the professionals to whom you are about to entrust yourself, before take-off.

That just about covers using Planesmanship to get on your way. But what about when you get there? If you are arriving in a foreign country or returning to the United States, you will have to go through the formalities of health and immigration checks. Your passport will be examined and stamped and your health documents scrutinized.

For entry into various countries, you will need certain inoculations. The requirements for these vary, and depend upon your points of flight origination and termination. Your travel agent or airline will be glad to provide you with details of health requirements, long before you take your trip. If by chance you do not have the necessary inoculations, most countries will give you your shots at the airport before passing you through. Some of the after-effects of these shots can make you feel out of sorts for a couple of days so I advise that you go through that experience at home and not in your expensive vacation hotel.

Having cleared health and immigration, you then proceed to the baggage pick up area. When your bags appear, check very carefully that they are indeed yours. It is a better than even chance that there is a duplicate of your suitcase in the mass of baggage off your flight. Before rushing off, check the identification tags you should have attached.

Almost all foreign airports have adopted a very efficient Red/Green customs procedure. If you have something to declare (lists of such items are available in the customs area) you should proceed through the area marked by large red signs. There, a customs officer will determine if and how much duty you must pay. If your belongings contain nothing which warrants examination, you may proceed through the Green customs area. In this area customs officers, both uniformed and plainclothed, may stop you and examine your baggage. In such an event if you are pure of heart and clear of conscience, you have nothing to worry about—or do you? Most people who are caught with something questionable, are totally unaware that they are carrying a restricted item.

The most common and embarrassing peccadillo I see

exposed is the carriage of forbidden books and magazines. The new wave of sexual freedom and honesty has yet to wash upon the shores of many foreign lands. Books and magazines, on open sale and display at respectable book-shops and newsstands in the United States, will blow the minds of customs officials in certain less enlightened countries. Spain and Portugal tend to be somewhat lacking in art appreciation and have overdeveloped prurient in-terests ready to be appealed to. The strictest place in the world for customs-applied censorship is, believe it or not, the land of new freedom, Australia. Although a stroll along any Australian beach would boggle the mind of a hardened pornographer, a copy of *Playboy* or *Penthouse* magazine will promptly be confiscated. They are passed among the customs officers to strengthen their resolve to remain a bulwark against such mind-destroying evil. These confis-cated publications are subsequently destroyed not by cleansing fire however; they usually fall apart after being passed from hand to hand!

Different countries get up-tight about different things. In England, for instance, your sexual idiosyncrasies elicit less attention than your smoking and drinking habits. To-bacco products and liquor in excess of the allowable amounts, usually 200 cigarettes and a fifth of liquor will be confiscated and locked away in the Queen's warehouse, to be later sold or destroyed.

If you are on an extensive trip which takes in more than one country, you may be carrying amounts of tobacco and booze in excess of that allowed in a particular country. You may request that the customs store the excess in a bonded warehouse and, for a small fee, collect them when you depart that country. If your stopover is less than 24 hours, you may also make use of the coin-operated lockers availa-ble in the customs areas of many airports.

If your personal inclinations run to drugs, hard or soft, I will offer one word of practical advice—Don't! Drugs are the hottest items in every customs division in the world. One ounce of "grass" will buy you room and board for a very long period of time. Unfortunately the appointments of your accommodation may be somewhat less comfortable than you anticipated at your hotel.

In the course of a year, I pass through hundreds of customs checks. Despite the purity of my heart and the clarity of my conscience, I always feel guilty as I pass the stony scrutiny of the customs officers. Despite what I know is a furtive look, I have rarely been stopped and searched. I do recall one occasion in Chicago, upon the termination of a flight from London, when I was hit by the "Black Gang."

The "Black Gang" is a term used by crew members to describe a team of customs officers assigned to perform minute searches of individuals and equipment. I discovered later, that on this occasion U.S. customs had received a tip-off that a large consignment of heroin was due in that day, smuggled in from Europe by a crew member. Having no information on which flight or even airline was supposed to be carrying the stuff, they gave the full treatment to every crew member arriving from Europe.

My hobby is cooking and my speciality is Indian curry. While in London I had purchased a quantity of spices from a specialty gourmet shop. The spices had been packed in plain unmarked cans. I had declared them on my customs' declaration form as "spices," and when my customs officer came upon the cans, apparently concealed in the bottom of my suitcase, his face lit up. Seizing the first can he opened the lid and was rewarded with the sight of the white powder it contained. Before I could stop him, he took a quick sniff at the open can. To say that he sneezed, would be an inadequate description of the explosion which occurred. Scattering the very hot spice about in his paroxysm of sneezing, he reduced the entire area into a shambles.

The search which I was subsequently subjected to was astonishing. I had no idea that my body and my baggage contained so many potential hiding places. I was "clean" and was released with apologies. I certainly bear no ill will about the episode; indeed, I am comforted by the professionalism and thoroughness of our customs service. Incidentally, later that day, a kilogram of pure heroin was discovered hidden in the brassiere of an Air France stewardess.

To expedite your passage through customs in the United States, make a list of all the items purchased overseas and attach the sales receipts. Pack those articles in one case if possible or at least near the top of your cases, so they may be found quickly if the customs officer wishes to examine them. Customs officers are perfectly human and appreciate any attempts you make to help them in their job. They are not out to nail the average once-a-year tourist who maybe fibs about the price of the new watch he bought in Zurich; their quarry is the professional or bigtime smuggler and the criminal who brings drugs into the country.

One last word of advice on customs: never, never take anything through customs for someone else. This dodge is as old as hiding contraband in your dirty laundry. I have a friend who struck up an acquaintance with a very pretty girl on a flight from Frankfurt. During the course of conversation, she ascertained that my friend had made no purchases overseas. As she had exceeded her duty-free allowance, she asked if he would take something from her and declare it against his own allowance. Unable to refuse a pretty girl such a reasonable request, he agreed, and accepted a large ceramic pig which he stowed in his carry-on bag.

At New York when a customs officer found a half-kilo of hashish inside the pig, my friend realized that he was in serious trouble. Fortunately his travelling companion had not yet passed through customs and he was able to convince the officer that he was carrying the pig for her. A search of her handbag revealed a sales slip for the pig and she broke down and confessed. My friend was released with a stern warning not to try such a thing again—advice which I am sure was totally unnecessary by then.

Having passed through customs unscathed, we are now on our own and ready to venture forth into a new city.

Every major airport I know in the world is located several miles from the downtown area of its adjacent city. Before letting your skycap or porter steer you to what may be a very expensive taxi-cab ride, check with a ground agent from your airline and find out the details of the bus service that is always available. Almost without exception I have found these bus services to be quick, frequent, convenient and cheap.

If you prefer to take a cab—agree on a price before the driver loads you and your baggage. I have found most cab drivers to be very honest, but it doesn't hurt to hedge your bet in case you run into one of the few who will figuratively as well as literally take you for a ride.

Paying the porter for carrying your baggage can be a difficult situation in a strange country. As a rule of thumb I suggest that if you gave him between 20 and 25 cents in local currency for each bag, you will not be undertipping or adding to that undeserved myth of the Ugly American.

While in the airport area, if you have any problem of any nature, such as hotel reservations, transportation, money exchange, etc., call upon a representative of your airline. He is a local person, able to speak the language and has been selected for his knowledge and helpfulness. He is ready to assist you.

Have you got all that? If you have, you are a master at the game I call Planesmanship. I guarantee, if you follow these suggestions to the letter, you'll have a happier, a more convenient, and above all, a cheaper trip!

Air travel is undoubtedly one of the most exciting "trips" going. It is as close to you as your nearest airport. Don't just use it—get into it and enjoy being part of it. The professional crew members are happy to share with you the adventure and fascination which it holds. Flying airplanes is not just a job for us—it is a way of life.

This is your captain speaking. Thank you for flying with me. Happy landings!